I0135994

Bar, Stage and Platform: Autobiographic Memories

Herman Charles Merivale

Contents

BAR, STAGE AND PLATFORM:

AUTOBIOGRAPHIC MEMORIES

BY

Herman Charles Merivale

BAR, STAGE, & PLATFORM

CHAPTER I
PALMERSTON AND OTHERS
WITH INTRODUCTORY MATTERS

" IN the first place, Mr. Merivale, where *are* the Colonies ? " How different it all seems now, with Australia "advancing" and Canada so near to us, and Imperial Institutes teaching the Anglo-Saxon legend. For it was the stout old British Premier, Lord Palmerston—most British of all the ministers of my time—who introduced himself to my father in those words in his room at the Colonial Office, where the last held the post of Permanent Secretary for many years from 1847 onwards. Lord John Russell was the Secretary for the Colonies under Palmerston, when he under-took a special mission to the Ionian Islands, and the Premier—committing himself in those days to no special post of his own, but overlooking things generally under the comfortable style of Chancellor of the Duchy of Lancaster—figured in Lord John's post himself for the time. And so it was that the airy and famous Minister introduced himself one morning. " Well, you hear that I've come to look after the Colonies myself now Russell's gone. In the first place, Mr. Merivale, where *are* the Colonies ? Glad to see that you've plenty of maps about." Maps and to spare there certainly were, ornamenting in huge rollers the official walls, and serving in place of pictures when drawn down. Many an hour have I spent there in my boy-days looking on them with awe, but not with profit, being one of the many who never could, and never can, get any ideas of geography except by visiting the places for myself. The fact that Malaga, till I went to that incomparable capital of health and climate to stay, lies as far south as the southernmost. point of Sicily, never assimilated itself to my mind. It seemed, rather, on a kind of vague level with the Riviera, at the other side of the blue-roofed Midland sea. I knew it from the map of course, but maps pass from my mental vision like so many dissolving views. So they did with Palmerston, he said, and I remember feeling that to be a great consolation, and giving up the geographic struggle from that moment "I manage the British Empire, as you know," he went on; " but I never could understand my latitudes and longitudes, or make out where the British Empire isn't." "Pain's" cheery manner and quick aptitude proved a great delight to my father, who always said that the main difficulty of a Per-manent Secretary lay in the changes of Government, and in always losing his chief just when he had mastered his business. Only too often the ministers appeared to be chosen on the Gilbertian principle made so renowned by *Pinafore,* of the square peg in the round hole, being told off to War, or the Colonies, or India as the case might be, as the men who knew least of their subject The choice appeared to be dictated either by the principle that their minds should be without prejudice at starting, or with a generous view of improving their education. But be that as it may, my father always said that half his time seemed to be spent in teaching his various chiefs their elements. It gave I him, however, a great opportunity of insight into character, and interested him from that standpoint very much. It was of Lord Grey, as one of his chiefs, that he said that his mind was like an elephant's trunk, which could pull up a tree or pick up a pin. After some years my father left the Colonial Office to take up the same post for India at the special request of the Indian Minister of the time, the Duke of Argyll. And I well remember his telling me that, while half the most noted ministers of his day passed through his quiet hands, as one of the un-acknowledged but working rulers of the unending show, no one of them ever so impressed him with his astonishing power of grappling at once with subjects new to him, and mastering in a moment all the details and proportions of the work, as Lord Salisbury, who was afterwards so fitly to develop into the most powerful of all the Prime Ministers of the latter part of the century. None of them since Pitt, I suppose, has held the position so securely for so long, in spite of the great democratic wave that has so merged the ancient landmarks; mainly, perhaps, because of it Lord Salisbury was but a very short time at the India Office, as it was near the occasion of his separation from Disraeli over the latter's Reform Bill, and my father never regretted any of his changes so much.

As Lord Robert Cecil, Lord Salisbury was a frequent guest at my father's house, and on terms of much personal friendship begun through his brilliant wife. It was as Lord Salisbury's guest at Hatfield that my father's long illness first struck him down. The daughter of Baron Alderson, the well-known and humorous judge of his day, Lady Salisbury was one of the most attractive women, from sheer talent and variety, whom I can easily recall. My father had been at the Bar like everybody else, and went the Western Circuit with the Cockburns and Edlins and others of the day, for that circuit was almost as famous as a nurse of judges, as "autocratic Balliol" of Oxford heads and scholars. In my turn I was to fall under the same spell and join the same circuit, though my irresistible and wandering propensities prevented my doing my obvious duty to the woolsack, or ever sticking absolutely to anything. But it is He that hath made us, and not we ourselves, I take it—and if I have been by turns something, I fear, of everything except a man of business—well, I cannot help it. My unlucky ignorance in the latter capacity was to prove a very Aaron's serpent on the threshold of old age, and swallow up the whole in one sudden ruin at a moment's notice, through the default of a trusted friend and solicitor, and left me at sixty years to begin nothing in particular, upon nothing at all. It has left me to reflect rather sadly that I never studied the Mammonic art of "beggar my neighbour," and haven't the vaguest notion how to cheat But after all, if everybody did that, there would be nobody to be cheated, and the fear would cease. Yet even in the matter of business, perhaps, I wrong myself I was an egg-merchant once, and as I couldn't do anything else to help the concern on in person, I wrote its advertisements in verse. Here is one, which strikes me now as quite entirely beautiful, and worthy of all that Pears or Colman can record :

Oh! know'st thou the land where the mighty St. Gothard
Is tunnelled and hollowed and corkscrewed away ?
The glacier quaked and the avalanche tottered,
When the railway trains came underneath them to play.
Once singers and painters fair Italy lent us,
Where now she provides us with coal and with beer;

But nothing so charming has Italy sent us
As, }*vid* St. Gothard, the eggs of Lemiere.

Hurrah for the march and the triumphs of Science,
Yoking Nature herself to the wheels of her car;
Now distance and time are both set at defiance,
And eggs for the million come smiling from far.
Italian and German and Frenchman and Paddy
All haste with their freshest and wholesomest here,
And the lad to his lass, and the lass to her laddie
Can bring for a present the eggs of Lemiere.

The hens cackle songs of delight when they lay them,
The customers dance when they come to the door;
So modest the bills, it's a pleasure to pay them,
For who could digest other eggs any more ?
Would you poach, would you boil, would you curry or roast 'em ?
In equally beautiful shapes they appear;
So sound and so sweet and so perfect we boast 'em.
You might live all your life on the eggs of Lemiere.

I always understood that this poem had a great effect on customers at the time. My connection with the firm didn't last very long, perhaps, for I fear that as I looked upon the ledger-side of eggs I did little but addle them. But I never walk through Clerkenwell without reflecting that I have done my whole duty as an Englishman, and that I was once in trade. I wish I had never left those eggs, for they are paying still, and when the census paper came round and my name was writ therein not as barrister, or author, or dramatist, or anything of that unworthy kind, but simply as egg-merchant, the pride that comes before a fall for once was mine. I was for once a respectable Englishman in trade.

In such a parlous strait as mine, autobiography seems a safe resource in the hands of a trustful publisher. And I am not the Methuselah I may seem, for I began remembering before I could write and read. I can remember now seeing the Duke of Wellington's funeral from those windows of my father's at the Colonial Office, while at what age I assisted at the Battle of Waterloo (at Astley's) in all the primitive "staging" of that day, with the French army drawn up on one side in blue, and the English army on the other in red, a cannon in front of every third combatant, discharged point blank into the persons of the other side, Napoleon himself in effigy in the presence of the famous Mr. Gomersal, and (as I think) a comic vivandiére performing prodigies of valour with the spent balls between the two armies—I cannot rightly remember. At something of the same date I must have made my first acquaintance with the legitimate drama at the successor of Foote's "little theatre in the Haymarket," and cowered in anguish before Macready's thunder in *King Lear.* He was a great tragedian I know, and discovered Helen Faucit, for which much may be forgiven him. But he did make a great noise from a small boy s point of hearing, and I heard him do it again afterwards as Hamlet, and reverse the situation by frightening the ghost. When, many years afterwards, my dear old Harrow friend and headmaster, Dr. Vaughan, sent a small page of his from

Doncaster to York to hear a famous preacher at the boy's particular request, he returned in the evening with a broad grin of delight upon his face. " Well, my boy, did you hear him well ? " asked the doctor. " Oh no, sir, I didn't hear him, but I see'd him a-hollering." Alas, that I should say it, but something of that memory returns on me still, when I think of the first of the many tragedians I have seen, and of what men called his school for some time afterwards. This is to digress indeed, but as my good old patron, correspondent, and publisher of happier days, George Bentley, used to say of me, digress I must. Digression is part of me whatever it may be worth. What readers I may find will accept mine as a roving commission, and remember that by my own confession I never stick to anything, in subject apparently as in other things. My pen must have its way, and follow its sweet will.

Lord Palmerston, again! How he comes back to me, and how I like to think that he spoke to me, like the small boy whom the Duke of Wellington d—d. I can remember him so well, in his vigorous old age, riding hard down the hot road in July to figure at the "speech-day" of his good old Harrow, and riding back again as soon as the serious function of the day was over—riding as men of business do ride, elbows out, toes in. Always the jovial Palmerston—the typical Briton of no large brain, but all the qualities of popularity; who in the temporary absence of the " big figures" won an almost absolute sway, out of his perfect sympathy with the average British mind. The "Palmerstonian Liberal" was not only a fact, but a lasting one. He hit the golden British mean exactly. And he has absolutely revived in the "Imperialist Liberal Unionist," that perplexing politician of the many names.

Well, I have seen him often in my younger days. I have presumed to argue with Gladstone about music, and even induced him to say that he "would take time to consider my proposition." I have been petted by Joanna Baillie, I have shuddered at Macready, I have listened to Macaulay, I have defended the Briton's character in America, just after the Civil War, alone against the wrath of Lowell and of Sumner3, I have loved and cherished the personal talk of Wendell Holmes—so like his exquisite writing—over Boston's choicest whaffles; I have watched Garibaldi playing bowls at Nice, I have listened in the same town to Clara Novello singing songs for me all by myself, in her little button of a house as she called it; I have listened to the philosophy of De Tocqueville, the Republicanism of Louis Blanc, the omniscience of Buckle, and the metaphysical theories of Manning, by hours at my father's table; I have edited and largely written that sound and wholesome work, the ***Annual Register,*** for ten mis-spent but patient years, I have indited prose and verse for ***Punch,*** and the ***Spectator,*** and the ***Saturday,*** and the ***World,*** and ***Truth,*** all at the same time. I have harangued a Church Congress, and an Art Society, and an Educational Institute, and political crowds unnumbered. I have acted many a time with Kate and Ellen Terry, and been the last of Helen Faucit's Touchstones when she bade the stage farewell. I have led cotillons night after night in the marble halls of fashion, in my day ; and loved my battles in the grand old tennis-courts of Paris, Brighton, Hampton Court, perhaps more in my heart than any other of my shifting scenes. I have been treated by Thackeray as a son, and Dickens as a friend and contributor. I have written tragedy for Irving, comedy for Toole, melodrama for Clayton, and burlesque for Hollings-head, after being taught the whole art of play-writing in an hour of vivid talk by the generous kindness of Dion Boucicault.I have walked long walks of talk with Vaughan at Harrow, and with Jowett at Oxford. I have sate at the feet and at the table of Hutton of the Spectator, wisest and kindest both of all men

I have known, and worked for him for nearly twenty years. I have been offered an Irish seat gratis by Parnell himself. I have been invited to fight Bristol against Beach, and Brighton against Marriott, as a full-fledged 1880 lunatic. I have contended on the Western Circuit in Coleridge and Karslake days, and have been joint-counsel for Government in the Court of Privy Council, amongst other cases in the famous story of Dyce Sombre. I have been a Boundary Commissioner in Wales, a Caucus in Sussex, a Chief Justice's Marshal, with Matthew Arnold for my colleague, a Private Secretary in Spain, and an egg-merchant in Clerken-well. I have adored my married home, and loved my library. I have lived amongst the Italian galleries, and stored my soul with art in Dresden and Madrid as well; so that any one who cares to go any further with me, on the strength of so rolling-stone an index, will expect to read the story of one who has done much by turns, and nothing long enough, who has rejoiced in dear close friends, if few, and had no small share of enemies where he should find them least, one, finally, in whom the bump of ambition has been so discreditably absent that I doubt if he has ever cared for anything so much as just to live his full and varied life in his own unchastened way. And that he did till the law said him nay; while except for a few pages culled from the Family Memorials about his pedigree, of which he remembered nothing and cared less, from first to last he has consulted throughout his book no single note-book for a word, except the pigeon-holes and store-houses of a rather remorseless memory.

CHAPTER II

ABOUT SOME FAMOUS FOLK IN MANY LINES

LORD TAUNTON, once Mr. Labouchere, was another of the Colonial Min-istersand friends of the Palmerstonian era whose names recall my first memories of the political world. The inevitable law of contrast often brings the solemn and rather starched figure to my mind, as one of my own earliest hosts at his place near Stoke Poges—so connected with that luckiest of poets, Gray, who was bequeathed to immortality on the strength of a single elegy. " Sir, he was a barren rascal," was all that Dr. Johnson could be induced to say of him. Uncle and precursor of our own more famous Labby, Lord Taunton is fabled to have lived in a general state of alarm at the strange proclivities of that unchastened heir, who has provided the world with more amusing stories, and more sayings of a curious humour, than any public man of his time. It is fabled that when Lord Taunton heard that his nephew contemplated public life, and proposed to stand, I think, for one of the county divisions in the district, he was much pleased at such a sign of grace, and asked if he could himself do anything for him. " Really, I think not, uncle," was the answer. " But I don't know. If you would put on your peer's robes, and walk arm-in-arm with me down the high streets of Windsor, perhaps it might have a good effect." My father, who partook by nature and training of the older methods, but had a considerable sense of silent fun to help him, was rather alarmed when the course of events brought the younger Labouchere, lately a diplomat and reputed to be the terror of the Foreign Office—as the hero of various anecdotes which, with a proper dread of "chestnuts," I shall avoid repeating here—to dine at his table. To me he was a stranger, but as the two juniors of the party we stood out as the two odd men, with no ladies to take down. As my father was apt to be oblivious of his social duties, and my mother, an invalid, unable to leave her carrying-chair, it was my duty, on those good old mahogany days of sitting over the wine and dessert, to pair off the guests together. As we followed in their wake, my companion quietly addressed me with, " Have you got that to do ? " I laughed, and said yes. " I wouldn't, if I were you. You'll find it a great bore." " But I can't help it" " Oh, yes you can ; I did. When I went to Madrid as junior attach^, I found it was my duty at the big dinners, and saw at once that that wouldn't do. So I stopped it at the first one. They're very particular about precedence and that sort of thing in Spain, much more than we are here. So I sent all the wrong people down with all the wrong people. And there was such a devil of a row."

My mind that evening was full of much anxious expectation. For some few months before Alfred Wigan, most polished of comedians of the day and the first great apostle of "reserved force," as it came to be called (which in itself was to be accounted a blessing in days when too much of the more prominent acting was like the lion's part in *Pyramus andThisbe,* nothing but roaring), had opened the Queen's Theatre in Long Acre, now converted into stores, with a little farce of mine by way of curtain-raiser, which brought me many golden guineas in ten weeks—more than my first three years at the bar were able to effect together. Thus early had I embarked on the drama's perilous sea, but only under a stage-name, my ***nom dttage,*** as a worthy actor of my acquaintance once called his "alias." If a barrister then wrote openly for the stage, ye gods! So Merry Vale was loosely translated into " Mr. Felix Dale," and faced the footlights for the first time, I think, somewhere about the year of grace 1865. But it was over my farce at the Queen's that I first quailed under the terrors of criticism, when a stern critic pierced my disguise, and lamented that a crude effort of reprehensible frivolity should have been perpetrated under a thin veil, which concealed the name of an " honoured official who had grown grey in the public service." My worthy father was suspected of having taken to evil courses at his advanced age, and written " He's a Lunatic " in secret. I must say that my worthy father enjoyed the joke very much, and so afterwards did the cruel perpetrator, who was to figure in later days as a warm friend and liberal manager of mine, John Hollingshead.

After that farcical prelude, Alfred Wigan tempted me into melodrama, and I first tried my stage wings seriously, still under my guilty alias, in partnership with my old friend and master of the arts of stage-construction, Palgrave Simpson. We did the plot, he did the construction, and I did the writing, the share in all my stage-work which, whether alone or in collaboration of plot and story, I have always kept jealously to myself. I never could quite believe in one play written by two hands, though many brains may combine to invent one. It is the writing that must form the characters; and I cannot see how any one, written by two, can possibly form a consistent reality. On the night of that dinner at my father's, the melodrama was just coming out. Wigan had a mysterious partner in management, to whom he had spoken of the disguised, but eminent author. Two or three days afterwards, I was sent in fear and trembling to the manager's room at the Queen's, to meet the mysterious partner. I was introduced, and sitting at the table with a cigarette in his mouth, I saw—Labouchere. " Good Lord ! " he said, "are*you* the eminent author ? " " Heavens!" quoth I, " are *you* the mysterious partner?" Both of us had carefully concealed our hidden sin at the dinner-party. What struck me most was a small array of bills of the new play hung all round, each printed with a different title, that the mysterious partners might see which looked best. It was, at all events, bold expenditure. *Time and the Hour* was the title that the authors had hit upon ; and Labouchere decided that it should be chosen. " It's a splendid title, I think," he said. "Delighted that you say so," was my flattered answer. "It really is, you know. Do for any play whatever that ever was written." And if you think of it, so it would. At this particular stage of my own life's drama, I realise it with a little pain.

Time and the Hour, as it turned out, was in its way a kind of curiosity. For the cast comprised, besides Wigan himself, a whole bouquet of coming managers, then all more or less at the beginning. There were "Johnnie" Toole, " Lal," or Lionel Brough. "Jack," or John Clayton, Charles Wynd-ham, and Henrietta Hodson, afterwards to be the wife of her new manager, who presented himself to her first behind the scenes before she knew of his position in the place, with the information that he wouldn't stay because he must be off to the shop. On her expressing some curiosity as to the nature of the establishment he kept, he blandly explained that he meant the House of Commons. No life has been much more double than Labouchere's, whose real personality none has exactly sounded. To this day his peculiar views, and yet more peculiar way of putting them, have made him a terror and a shaking of the head to a large section of the world, as doubtless to his uncle at the outset. But a more delightful companion, a quieter and more gentle soul, a more attractive host, or a kindlier mortal, might be looked for throughout the ranks of the accepted all in vain. Like his contemporary Irving, he seems to be perpetually surveying everything with a sense of puzzled wonder why he himself particularly "came off," and what the whole business, as far as he is con-cerned, happens to be about Irving, by the bye, when only selected by the few as likely to figure in the front rank, was also in the field with *Time and the Hour,* not as a player in the piece, but as stage-manager. And characteristic was my first meeting with him, not over the drama, but over some little farce of mine which was put into rehearsal, but for some reason not produced. One of the characters was a servant-maid with nothing much to do. On to the stage bounced a very handsome and full-blown young woman gorgeously costumed, who proclaimed without delay, " I will consent to play this part, if the author will write me in a young man." Irving and I observed her, I with astonishment, he with his regardful smile. " Quite so, my dear," he said, "

I'm afraid the author will not be able to do that without disturbing the balance. You know, the balance. But I'm sure that if you're good and do your best, he will give you some riddles to ask." The lady was to blossom at the music-halls as Miss Kate Santley. The heroine of *Time and the Hour* was winsome Nelly Moore, the Ada of Sothern s *David Garrick,* and most sympathetic of English ingénues. *Charles Wyndham contented himself with a few rehearsals, and with precocious independence of his authors threw up his part; one of his first in London, I think. He had to figure as the* jeune pre-mier, *and couldn't stand it. I cannot blame him, and even then I did not. When I think of the sort of parts that used to be written in that long-suffering line in those days, remorse gnaws me as it did the American defaulter. As an amateur actor, slim of figure, candid of appearance, and romantic of mind, I was always being cast for the horrid things myself. It must have been in revenge I wrote them. To appear as* a.jeune premier was to be scouted for a " stick." I never shall forget the suffering of enacting Faulkland to the capital Sir Anthony of the prince of amateur actors, Sam Brandram, afterwards the famous Shakespearean reader, the Bob Acres of Quinten Twiss, and the David of Arthur Blunt, who was to become the same universal favourite on the stage as off it as Arthur Cecil. I forget the name of my " Julia," entirely. But two-thirds of our two parts were very properly cut out, and we suffered silently together in the noble cause of amateur acting.

Of a very different and more orthodox type were most of the guests who gathered at my father's table. Macaulay, with his rich talk and rare flashes of silence, came a good deal from the house of his sister, Lady Trevelyan, who lived at neighbour's distance three or four doors off. The first meeting with him that I can remember, however, was on board a Rhine boat, when he discoursed so largely and learnedly about all things to my listening parents that I slunk away, small creature that I was, and, seated on the paddle-box, embarked upon my first flight of verse, in the shape of a transfation of

Sie sollen ihn nicht haben
Den freien Deutschen Rhein,

under the straightforward guise of

Oh no, they shall not have it
The free and German Rhine.

At this distance of time it does not, I confess, sound as if it had been written under the inspiration of Macaulay and his ringing Roman ballads. My parents were very indignant with me for my want of appreciation, but the great man was a little out of my infant depth, I own. Yet to this day I can recall the full deep talk, and the knowledge which seemed to leave out nothing. It is a great mistake of the present day, surely, to underrate him. The ballad-poets of the world are very rare, from Homer—whether he was one or many, according to the @@@X<*>piZ6vreg@@@ or their foes—down to Macaulay's day. As to the great Greek father of the ballad-child, there are cases where internal evidence is stronger than all laboured proof; and that Homer was a Ballad Com- pany, Limited, passes my power of personal be-lief. Not Walter Scott himself made greater use in his verse of the music of sonorous names.

Sempronius Atratinus
Sate at the western gate

pairs off in my memory with

Sir David Lindsay of the Mount,
Lord Lyon King-at-Arms,

while the incomparable march of the address of the great Twin Brethren would take a great deal of more aesthetic beating:

By many names men call us,
In many lands we dwell;
Well Samothracia knows us,

Cyrene knows us well.

There is something in the as *rotundum* yet, surely, and Sound has a greatness of its own, when it doesn't mean mere Fury. No English patriotic verse, a difficult weapon to handle, has ever surpassed the noble fragment that Macaulay called "The Armada." No master of English, in prose and verse as he was, is ever to be despised, for they are the Makers of the Language in its purer and enduring forms. And the little critics are never so little as when carping at the few big men. The rest are fair game, no doubt But when a superfine artist in that line of late years took to rating Macaulay for beguiling a rough passage between Holyhead and Dublin by repeating to himself a list of the Popes, or the first book of the ?neid, or some other of the miscellaneous treasures of his mental store-house, instead of " thinking out the Irish problem " as was his business at the time, the disproportion of the thing was a little depressing. Supposing Macaulay to have been as sea-sick as even the greatest of men may be, his reflections on the Irish question would scarcely have been profound in value.

From the real omniscience to the spurious is an easy step of memory, and Macaulay and Buckle, the Historian of Civilisation, a lion of a season, stood at the two poles of omniscience. Buckle was a very omniscient lion indeed, a very lion in buckram, on a night when I remember his dining at my father's, and he laid down the law on anything and everything with a magnificent pomposity which made the table quake. He roared after a manner of his own, equally remote from the sucking dove and the nightingale. I gaped merely, having all my life been of the ill-informed, they say, because I have written plays. My father listened, as he slowly sipped his sherry after the fashion of the day, with a tiny twinkle in his eye familiar to those who knew him best, when he had a pretender to deal with. He never answered them, but only "took stock," and he had a quick way of his own of distinguishing the false from the true. Unluckily for Buckle he had a listener of another kind in Lyulph Stanley, of School Board fame, a contemporary and Balliol ally of my own in those days, of whom Lowell once said to me in America that he "knew three times as many facts as any young man whatever had any business to know." He had but one rival in that line, Frank Palgrave of the "Golden Treasury," and much interest was aroused amongst their friends when the two once departed on a tour together. It was even betting which would return alive. When they did return, Palgrave was pale, emaciated, silent; Stanley in incomparable form, and fitter far than ever. He was a queer customer for Buckle that night. He listened as respectfully as he could, as long as he could. Only intervals of a slight shaking of the head, and of a slight redness of the face, suggested the shortcomings of the great master of inaccuracy. At last Buckle made some statement about the latest burning of a witch, and the date of the performance, some hundred years or more too far back, Stanley could stand it no longer, but fairly got on his feet, extended his right hand, and in a vigorous treble spoke: " I beg your pardon, the last witch was burned at such-and-such a place, in such-and-such a year, under such-and-such circumstances. And her name was so-and-so, and you will find all about it in a book to which I can easily refer you, which you evidently don't know." And torrents of imprisoned knowledge were poured on Buckle's head, till the historian of civilisation sate wrathful, extinguished, mute. He had his revenge later on, in a form which is not to be forgotten. Somebody mentioned a new dictionary, and said it was a good one. " It is," said Buckle with much solemnity, having had time to recover from Stanley's onslaught. "It is one of the few dictionaries I have read through with pleasure." I have always remembered that as the most appalling utterance of my day. The idea of a man who read through dictionaries for a relaxation, and enjoyed some of them, is a little difficult to improve upon.

A Stanley of another kind, though of the same race, was Arthur Stanley, the famous Dean of Westminster, who once said that his knowledge of music was confined to two tunes, one which was " God Save the Queen," and another which wasn't As Jenny Lind was his father's protégée and his own early friend, the special ignorance had its odd attraction. He was the best talker of his time, one perhaps who said nothing to be especially remembered or recorded, but was always bright and varied, attractive, scholarly, and entertaining. He took as well as gave, being an admirable listener, and as my father, though naturally a silent man, talked in a very interesting fashion when he did talk, they could make a table very pleasant between them. Arthur Stanley bore a curious resemblance to Wendell Holmes, most fascinating and human of American men of letters, in the likeness of his talk and his writings. The writings were not great in Stanley's case, but so gentle, so historical, so casually poetic. And the same graceful fancies filled his talk. Manning, a divine of another kind, before his more famous days in the purple, was a great deal at our house in Westbourne Terrace. He had been my father's pupil at Oxford; and though between the Oxford tutor and pupil the distance of years is often very small, the distance in reverence is rather overpowering. University pupils always remember their tutors as men of a patriarchal age. The famous Cardinal loved to sit at one of my father's feet while I reposed at the other. He never came to dine, because from the earliest hours of life he was possessed of the most boundless " scruples " on the matter of digestion. As if man was not omnivorous, and obliged to eat. To many it is not entertaining, but has to be done. But Manning would never dine, and as far as I know never did. He came for a cup of tea afterwards. He always had the greatest fascination for me from his kindliness, his " ewigweiblich-keit," his sweet simplicity of mind. He and my father had been nearly drowned together . on the Lake of Geneva in the Balliol days. " I never knew in all my life," it is recorded in Purcell`s " Life " that Manning said of his friend, "a man so ready of speech, or possessed of such intuitive knowledge as Herman Merivale." My father loved him, but never could quite believe in his pupil's depth. Manning, as many have learned since, was always the merest child on all questions of metaphysics, and sincerely believed them to be his strong point All his strong sympathies with right, and with the dim and common populations, which were to make him afterwards so great a favourite and so remarkable a figure, rose partly from that very metaphysical failure. In the after days, I always remember how one of my truest and strongest friends, the greatest journalist and most all-round brain of my time, Hutton of the ***Spectator,*** to whom metaphysics were as the life-blood of his heart, the metaphysics of religion especially, never could, did, or would " see anything " in Cardinal Manning but a lovable and amiable weakness, and a greatness that to him was rather accidental. Cricket was one of the great Cardinal's early distinctions, which seems somehow as inappropriate as the fact that John Morley's Oxford eminence was chiefly won in amateur theatricals. But Manning was also a boxer; and one of the younger priests who was trained under him has told me that, when he grew demonstrative in the pulpit, he had a knack of throwing his body backwards, and assuming the pugilistic attitude One thing at our house always amused me, the fact that my father kept and cherished two or three volumes of the Anglican sermons of the strenuous convert, which, with other reminders of his "days before the flood," he wanted to see burnt at the stake. He was always wanting to get them back, in vain. " No, thank you, Manning," was the constant answer.

The first Lord Lytton, another underrated figure of the past—chiefly because he was as much flayed alive by the criticisms of Thackeray as Charles Kean by Douglas Jerrold, as " Satan Montgomery" by Macaulay, as Colley Cibber by Pope— dramatist and novelist, poet, satirist, and politician all in one, whose abounding fertility of invention was in itself a strength—had been another of my father's Co-lonial chiefs, and was another of his guests and friends. His great deafness always seemed to throw him more back into his mental reserves. When my father wrote a book of various essays upon the higher subjects of the day, Lord Lytton wrote him a long letter of pure criticism, favourable and unfavourable both, which so deeply impressed its receiver that he begged the writer to publish it, and often told me how much it struck him that Lord Lytton might have figured as well as a critic as in every other line, had he chosen to turn his mind to it Lord Lytton had no train-ing as a dramatist But he wrote three plays which to this day hold their own better than any since Shakespeare, Sheridan, and Gold-smith. It is easier for the moderns to abuse their language, than to imitate their humanity and skill. He wrote a very wilderness of novels. But so completely did he grasp the difference between the two great branches of fiction, that he never " dramatised " any one of them, though oth-ers have done it for him over and over again. After my father's death, Lord Lytton's son, the ambassador and viceroy, sent me a short note found among his father's papers, saying that in his experience he had known " two brains of pure gold"— Macaulay's and my father's. But Macaulay's, he added, was as the gold beaten out into strips, my father's like "gold in the block." A son may perhaps be forgiven for reproducing that testimony to a strong but much too retiring figure. My father's ut-ter absence of all worldly ambition, and strange but abiding sense of the "Vanity of Vanities' were in the worldly sense his bane, not for himself only.

CHAPTER III

OF THACKERAY AND OTHERS

AMONG the legal figures wont to meet at my father's table, the Earles and Aldersons and Montagu Smiths and others, I think that with the exception of the first, who once took me round the Norfolk circuit in the pleasant sinecure of judge's marshal, I remember but the strong figure of Bethell, afterwards Lord Westbury, with the finical speech, like Digby Grand's in the *Two Roses,* sharply contrasted with the vigorous and uncompromising brain which made him so terrible an opponent. He was a kind of embodiment of pure logic, which is often apt to sweep away weak law like chaff before the wind, and results in a contempt for precedents apt to be very disturbing to the average legal mind. The bitter contempt with which he liked to annihilate in a single pithy sentence any inferior being who presumed to argue in his presence might have matched Carlyle's, whose crushing remark to Allingham, a gentle and amiable poet and man of letters, and sometime editor of *Eraser's Magazine,* always struck me as the greatest of recorded triumphs in that line. During the usual afternoon walk of which Allingham was one of the constant companions, holding his tongue most cautiously the while, Carlyle propounded some theory so startling that the gentle spirit rebelled, and went so far as to say, " Oh, Mr. Carlyle." Carlyle only checked him with a frown, and when they arrived at the steps of his house, instead of asking him to the usual cup of tea, looked at the poet steadily and said, " Young mon, let me tell ye that ye have within ye the capahcitee of becoming one of the greatest boares in the kingdom." And so dismissed him.

In the matter of logic, Westbury's armour was more difficult to pierce than that of the Chelsea sage, who ought to have been a dramatist by rights, and would have been magnificent, much as it would have shocked him to be told so, in his contempt for such trivialities. Carlyle's word-pictures are like those of great historic plays, and in many respects about as correct He would not have gone as far as M. Sardou, and repre-sented the moral Robespierre, who was guillotined at thirty-three, as being shot when the father of a very fine illegitimate son of apparently forty-five. But the playwright's liberties would have delighted him, and given him a field in which his full-blooded imagination would have been quite at home. To write of Lord Westbury is to be afraid of chestnuts—" dolls," as we used to call them in our circle, because of a West Indian custom of which a Drury cousin told us of dressing up dolls and shaking them when anybody transgressed. It was really at my father's table that he made his famous remark when somebody was made a judge over somebody else's head. "Really, he had a pimple, but I never knew it came to a head." Another time, when my father and he had both been listening in silence to some vocable talker laying down the law, Westbury quietly observed, when the gentleman was at last gravelled for lack of matter, " I don't think, Merivale, thai I ever heard such reasoning as that,. except from a country clergyman." The country clergy provided for some unknown reason Westbury's favourite tiltingground. But his wit, like Douglas Jerrold's, was generally rude and often brutal; and I confess to a personal preference for the summer lightning to the forked, in that line, of the kind one can associate with two such kindly humorists as Henry Byron and Frank Burnand. Playwrights, both I fear, Mr. Carlyle, like so many of the most dangerous and unchastened libertines of the pen. I t is a curious fact to be noted, none the less, that the editors of *Punch* from the first-a literary institution if ever there was one- have one and all been in succession dramatists, Mark Lemon, Shirley Brooks, Tom Taylor, Frank Burnand. A later personal memory, and very characteristic, of the famous Lord Chancellor, comes back to my mind in this connection. He was sitting as one of the Privy Council Judges in the famous" Dyce-Sombre" case, in which I had a junior brief for the Crown. In the lower courts he had once been the Begum Sumroo's counsel, and in the Court of Appeal he didn't forget it, acting much more like an advocate than a judge the whole time, when the chance offered itself. Of course he should not really have been present in the judicial capacity; but such details never troubled him much, I fancy. In the course of a nervous and youthful, but as I thought forcible, argument, I pointed out that at one time when the notori- ous lady (who once distinguished herself by burying an in-convenient slave alive under the chair in which she was sitting, and listening to the moans) was complain- ing of utter poverty, she was in receipt of a large pension from the Government. " Do you mean to advance that as a serious argument ? " said Westbury. " Yes, my lord" (tremblingly), " I do." " Really? Do you suppose that if I were in receipt of an income derived from a Government, and could double it by suppressing the fact, I should for a moment hesitate to do so?" The high-comedy tone of it was superb; and the proper repartee would, I suppose, have been, " No, my lord. I suppose *you* wouldn't." But if it rose to my dramatic lips, it didn't pass them.

Another terror of my Privy Council days was another great lawyer, and another of my father's guests, Sir Roundell Palmer. He had declined every judicial position possible by turns, the Lord Chancellorship included. The lesser lights that twinkled round the Privy Council table as his "judges" were all afraid of him. Judge then what a nervous junior must have been, who always dreaded speaking anything that he felt he could write very much better, except during a brief interval of political lunacy which rose with me out of the 1880 earthquakes. During that period, spouting on platforms was my delight and pride. I never could understand how I should suddenly have turned into a speaker. But once I had to speak for a deputation in the local county court, to commissioners seated on the bench above me. And at once the old legal shivers seized me, and to the astonishment of my admirers I utterly broke down on some purely commonplace question of business. Then I realised that there is all the difference between addressing an audience sitting above you, and an audience sitting below. I wouldn't address a bench of judges now for the world But place me on Sunium's marble step in the shape of getting into a witness-box, and being innocent I am happy. The terrors of the sharpest advocate do not impress me in the least, unless the judge is deaf, and everything has to be repeated. Then it becomes perplexing and a bore. In the Privy Council we all sat on a level, and the judges had no wigs on. So it was less terrible, but not by any means seductive. But to Sir Roundell Palmer. He led against me more than once, when I held a Government brief. When my leader had opened his case, and Sir Roundell had opened his, that leader was apt to depart rather timorously and unkindly, as I thought, and leave me to demolish the great man's arguments in reply. Sir Roundell at once went to sleep in his chair, seraphically, as if I were quite beneath his notice. So I was, but I never could see why my case and my clients should be. However, I was only too thankful to get through as best I might, not under the influence of that steely but observant eye. But I soon found out, that if I did happen to advance an argument of any value, he had a knack of waking as quietly as he slept, looking at the judges, shrugging his shoulders with a sad effect of pity, and going to sleep again. It was like Sheridan's " Lord Burleigh." Then the judges would all look at me and shake their heads, as who should say, " How dare you contradict Sir Roundell Palmer ? " Everybody knows the really great and good qualities of Lord Selborne. But the best of us has his weaknesses, I suppose; and perhaps his came out in his free use of the arts of advocacy. At least I remember some other grandee saying of him that it was "a grand thing for Palmer that he's such a great advocate. It's such a magnificent outlet for his fallen portion of natural dishonesty." I hope never to set down aught in malice, but I hate to " extenuate " a good thing away. And I never could arrive at any sense of proper appreciation of Lord Selborne's attitude in declining to act as Lord Chancellor for a Government who were going to disestablish a church, and accepting the same office under the same Government when they had disestablished it Surely, "your sin remaineth" The moral of Lord Westbury's fall, when he had to resign the Woolsack because of the misdemeanours of his eldest son, which parentally he had tried to shield, was told in a quaint saying, rightly or wrongly, attributed to the Queen. His successor, who had been passed over by right of Westbury's masterful power, was an eminently pious but uninteresting man. "You see, my lord," her Majesty was fabled to observe on giving him the seals, " how much better it is to be good than clever." There lurked much of unacknowledged humour in that Over-Sovereign, by right of character, of all the Sovereigns of Earth. If there was a weak spot in her armour at all, it was in her neglect of Ireland. At the very last moment, and in the very sight of death, was ever error of the judgment, not the heart, so touchingly and beautifully redeemed? She has made kinghood difficult, *the* Queen. As to her sense of humour, when somebody asked her if it was because of his politics that she didn't get on with Gladstone, she answered, " Not at all. It's because he will insist on addressing me as if I were a public meeting." To those who remember Gladstone upon Churches and States, it is the man in a dozen words.

Among the literary guests who rallied to our various round table, the central figure in my memory, as to me it must remain the kindliest and greatest, is always Thackeray's. I do not know, I cannot know, of any man who leaves with those who had the privilege that I had of intimacy as close as could be possible for one of another generation, such an abiding memory of an unqualified respect and love. He was not what is called a ''brilliant talker,'' and he was by some reputed to be bitter. He suffered enough, from losses and consequent desertion, to embitter any man, heaven knows! but I never remember a single sign of it. His talk as I recall it was all of kindness, gentleness, and sympathy ; and every action of his was the same.It was possible to be prejudiced, no doubt, in favour of my prose Shakespeare, the untouched god of my literary idolatry. We can all discuss and think about our hundred books or favourite novels: prefer " Ivanhoe " or the "Heartof Midlothian" according totaste—contrast " Monte Cristo " and the " Three Musketeers "—weigh the merits of " Nicholas Nickleby" and "Martin Chuzzlewit," or of the " Mill on the Floss " and " Adam Bede," and love or resent, according to the taste, " Emma" and " Pride and Prejudice." And we can speak in terms of reverence of " Tom Jones " and '' Roderick Random' even though we find them as hard to read through as that famous work, which everybody when asked about the true course of study mentions first and reads last, Gibbon's industrious classic But surely no one man in the world ever wrote four such masterpieces as "VanityFair," "Pen-dennis," " Esmond," and "The Newcomes." Trollope said of the first three, at the time of Thackeray's death, that all the world agreed about them, as a whole, but that the general public preferred " Vanity Fair," the critics "Esmond," and personal friends "Pendennis." Well, my own weakness is perhaps for " Pen " and George Warrington, at least I turn to them the oftenest; and Pen's proposal to Laura at the end is the shortest, truest, and most touching that hero ever made or heroine said " yes" to. And if Laura had the failings some attribute to her (she is an ideal English girl to me), the fashion of her acceptance should redeem them all. But the other three epics are none of them far behind. All four appeal to me before any others, whatsoever. The true delight of the novel which one knows by heart is that one can turn to any page of it at any time, and read as much or little as he needs. " Style " is the lord of letters, say what you will, and there is a restful. sense of company in Thackeray's which defies analysis. In one sense, it is no style at all. It suggests no effort. It gives no handle to imitation. The man can be as dramatic as Scott, as scholarly as Newman, as humorous as Dickens, as gossipy as Montaigne, as poetical as Ruskin, as strong as himself. The thing was done, but no critic upon earth can ever say how. Thackeray loved to have the young about him. Once when he asked me to dine with him at the little old Garrick Club in Covent Garden, before the mansion rose hard by, I had to plead that a Balliol friend was staying with me, who afterwards blossomed into an Egyptian judge. At once he asked him too, and carried us off afterwards to "Queen Victoria's own theayter" in the New Cut, where I first made acquaintance with villains as they should be, though I have of late discovered that they make no approach whatever to villains as they really are. Thackeray bent his silver head (for it was not white but silver) over the dress-circle, though dress was scarcely its characteristic. A gentleman from above took aim at it and spat thereon. Thackeray had quiet recourse to his silk handkerchief without looking up. " The gods are expectorating," he said; "something has gone wrong on earth." Some years afterwards I reminded him of that dinner, and asked if he remembered it " Of course I do," said he. " I gave you beefsteak and apricot omelette." Pride was not the word that we should have so impressed him. "Yes," he went on, patting my shoulder, and beaming through the well-known specs., " I always give boys beefsteak and apricot omelette." And I fell. Thackeray himself proposed me for the Garrick, and my seconder was Millais, always a cheery friend to me on my own account. But Thackeray died before the election, and Trollope, at his own request, took his place, so that I may plume myself on a good trio of sponsors. But it's an odd world. Just before the event I got an anonymous letter of warning to tell me that I was going to be " black-balled " by an enemy on the committee and had better withdraw. At the Garrick it was a case of committee election. But I got wroth, and wouldn't withdraw. I wrote at once to my proposer and seconder, who demanded the wherefore in committee. My foe turned out to be the Irish editor, or subeditor, of an evening paper, whose name I never heard of, and face I didn't know. It appeared that I had given him grave offence a few years before, by being " disrespectful" to him at some function of the "Old Stagers" at Canterbury, and that he felt I should not belong to the same club as he. He was obliged to withdraw his opposition in the face of such champions as mine. But for that friendly warning, as it proved to have been, he would have succeeded, and I should have been " black-balled " at the Garrick in spite of Thackeray, Trollope, and Millais without ever knowing why. That is how "black-balling" is done.

Thackeray's love of the stage was proverbial. " Don't you love the play ? " he asked a friend, " Yes, I like a good one." " Oh, go away, you don't understand what I mean." He loved the footlights and the baize and the whole illusion as Charles Lamb did, when the theatre became to him, " on a new stock, the most delightful of recreations." He liked to be there at the beginning and to sit it out, which meant something when one took a seat in the old Haymarket pit at half-past six, the best point of view from which a play was ever to be seen, and stayed all ears and eyes for two shillings, till past twelve, before suburban trains were, when the principal scenes were all acted in the middle instead of at the sides, where only two-thirds of the audience can see, and in cheery brightness instead of unmeaning darkness as they are now, always off the stage and often on it; when playbills could be comfortably studied and pleasant faces comfortably watched; and the entire action didn't give the impression of taking place at night Art it may or may not be, but it's very dull, and makes more friends for the music-halls, instead of the theatres, than managers seem to calculate or guess. Light is so great a blessing in a twilight world. But Thackeray could never write a play, though, as with so many novelists, it was to him a great ambition. His books never lent themselves to the treatment Scott, Dickens, and Lytton were always being dramatised, but Thackeray's work baffled the playwrights. I am not aware of a single play that has been made of it[1] Once at a manager's earnest solicitation I promised to write a comedy out of "Vanity Fair." I tried my best, but my scheme, when I had completed it, seemed to myself a cross between sacrilege and idiotcy. So I declined to go on. Once the great man wrote a two-act comedy for Alfred Wigan, then managing the Olympic, but Wigan found it impossible. He assured me that it was only because it would have been a mere success of curiosity, good enough for him, but likely to damage such a name as Thackeray's to no purpose. But Thackeray, he said, never quite forgave him. So we got up the Wolves and the Lamb ourselves, and acted it for a house-warming at the novelist's last house in Kensington Palace Gardens. Quinten Twiss and myself, Follett Synge, long our Consul at Hawaii, Morgan John O'Connell, one of Thackeray's hangers-on and the Liberator's brother, as a large footman with large calves, Sir Charles Young, who combined play-writingwith the Church Union, a daughter of Cole of the Brompton Boilers, a vulgar name now buried under the stateli-ness of the South Kensington Museum, Mrs. Caulfeild, afterwards Lady Charle-mount, and the host's younger

---

1   This sentence was written before the recent production of ***Becky Sharp.***

daughter, Minnie, who became Leslie Stephen's wife, made, with a few others, the "exceptional cast" It was grand fun for the actors, I remember. About the audience I don't know. Anyhow the two sides of the footlights were on such familiar terms, that when Synge, as the ne'er-do-weel, lighted a huge cigar and began to smoke it, a fine lady in the front row of the stalls, after a little sniffing, rose in her seat and said she hated tobacco, and hoped he would put it out He did; but he grew very hot and uncomfort-able, forgot his words, and added the prompter to the persons of the drama in an emphatic form. Thackeray himself declined a speaking part, but came on at the end as Mr. Bonnington, a very benevolent clergyman, and blessed us all in pantomime, audience included, while one member of the company recited some verses the novelist had written for the occasion. It was like Bellew reciting Hamlet, with dumb-show figures doing the business at the back. Thackeray's chief delight was in the play-bill, which he drew up himself, insisting on heading it with:

W.M.T. (EMPTY) HOUSE THEATRICALS.

For better than all the witticisms of Sheridan and Congreve he loved a bad pun at any time. That was a very bad one, and we all protested. But he would have it And he equally insisted on winding up his pet bill with :

N.B.—During the whole of this performance the theatre will *not* be perfumed by Rimmel's Patent Vaporizer.

It was the craze of the day in the fashionable theatres to diffuse this aromatic odour. Advertisement, now so wildly adult, was then in its infancy. WhenFechter, the Frenchman, opened the Lyceum, he scattered it with much generosity, and had decorated his ceiling with a clever imitation of lace. " Dear me!" said the witty and handsome actress, Miss Herbert, on his opening night, "the house is like a scent-bottle, and the roof like an antimacassar."

It was at that house in Palace Gardens that I remember, amongst many and many a happy evening, there congregated Brook-fields and Pollocks, and Theodore Martins, and Collinses, the brother of Wilkie Collins married to Charles Dickens's pretty and winsome daughter, Kate—always, with the brother-novelist, an especial favourite and child—and other memorable folk. I was seated at a man's dinner between Leech the artist and Sothern the comedian, and regarded both with a kind of gladsome awe. Sothern was then in the first flush of the wonderful "Dundreary," perhaps the most finished specimen of the imitative side of his art, before he exaggerated it too much, that the stage of our time has seen. It was really the actor's creation, a word which, as a rule, should be the author' s property. For Tom Taylor had made but a sketch of it in the writing as a very minor character. But it so tickled the fancy of the public in Sothern's hands, that with Taylor's full consent he developed it into the famous eccentricity. Sothern was then young, fair, and good looking, and very shy and refined in manner. He had begged Thackeray to ask him to meet Leech, and warmly expressed to the artist, across me, his gratitude to the " maker of his fortunes." Leech was puzzled, and Sothern explained how a constant study of his " smiles" in *Punch,* had filled him with the idea that they might be made to live upon the stage. He was in New York at the time, at Laura Keene's theatre. And when - she asked him as a favour to take the little part of Lord Dundreary in the comedy of *Our American Cousin,* written for Jefferson (" Rip Van Winkle "), he saw his chance and agreed, on the condition that he might dress it and " make it up" in his own way. And so the living Leech sprang into existence, first to take New York by storm, and afterwards London.

It must have been on the same evening that I expressed some youthful admiration of James Anderson's Orlando. He was a very handsome man, Macready's *jeune pre-mier,* but a real " roarer/' When in his advanced years he was asked to return to the stage, and play Antony to the Cleopatra of Miss Wallis at Drury Lane, it is said that he hesitated at first, fearing that his articulation was not what it used to be. But he took lodgings at Margate, and tried his voice upon the sands. When he found that he was audible at Ramsgate, he came back and played the part I heard him. Thackeray beamed at me at once in his dear old fatherly way, and quietly laughed "At last," he said, " I have seen a boy "—(to him I was always that)—"who admires James Anderson. I felt I must, some day." Not long afterwards he came to tea with me at the chambers where I was then living, in Garden Court—bringing with him the gracious Lady Colvile, whose husband was one of my Privy Council judges, afterwards. And it was with much pleasure to himself, and needless to say to me, that he identified the rooms with the very scene of one of his famous Temple episodes.

Once I wandered under Thackeray's wing through the exhibition of 1862, a tawdry, un-inviting show of industry and ugliness, I thought But I have had the same feeling about all these Mammoth Meetings, I confess, ever since the fairy realisation of Pax-ton's dream in glass and iron, in 1851. It was the strange new beauty of the thing, not its commercial trumpet-blowings before the strut of Progress, that left that first and last of the " Great Exhibitions " so peerless and alone. Of the modern additions to the Seven Wonders of the World, none ever passed the Chatsworth gardener's. It impressed itself doubly upon my memory, because I saw it opened on the morning of May 1, and in the afternoon was des-patched to Harrow, to enter the lists of life as a public school-boy, for the first time. The "quarter" had begun a week before, but my father kept me at home for that space, because he thought it good for me to have a chance that was not likely to come my way again. And the effect of that colossal and transparent "transept" has abided with me ever since. It was the Triumph of Beauty, not of Commerce, which glorified the reign of Peace, just three years before it was converted once again into the deadly and everlasting rebellion of war. In 1862 exhibitions had become "business," and business is not beautiful. Thackeray's mind brought its own beauty to bear on it, or I should remember nothing of the hideous monster at all. As we wandered down an uninteresting street of shops, each shoppier than its neighbour, but supposed to be remark-able for something not in evidence, we met a school of little girls in grey, with very wide-open eyes indeed, improving their harmless little minds under their mistress's guidance, in a quaint row of two-and-two. Thackeray stopped when he saw the little maidens, and they stopped too, and bobbed. " How many little girls are there?" he asked the mistress. " Four-and-twenty, sir." ''Four-and-twenty little girls." "They must have four-and-twenty little sixpences, to buy four-and-twenty little things with." And the procession was stayed till he had got all the change for himself and himself deposited a bright sixpence in every tiny hand The eight-and-forty eyes grew very large and bright, and the chorus of " Thank you, sir," very sweet and general. Then the procession passed, and so did we.

Thackeray talked to me more than once after that of some of the sweet corners and troubles of his life, in a way which endeared him to me more and more, from its touching and generous confidence.

He died suddenly not long afterwards, at Christmas-tide, the time I think when he must have wished to die, with that strange deep Calvary-faith of his. Nothing more hauntingly religious has ever been written down than the death of Helen Pendennis. He was a fighting-soldier in the Battle of Life, and had a horror of his own of the " Thomas a Kempis " school. But as many men, so many minds. And so alone can the great problem work itself out, as for itself it must I was to have dined with him, that Christmas Day, and learned the news in Devonshire, where once I had heard him lecture on the "Four Georges," in his own irregular but most absorbing way. That death eclipsed, indeed, the literature of nations. I know what it eclipsed for me. There has been a " boom in Thackeray," they say, of late. I am glad there has been. I am a hero-worshipper myself, so my gods are very few. Let the few demi-gods be boomed wherever we can find them. I hate the little carpers at the great man's heels. Anthony Trollope was never a great man on his own account, though a clever one. But not the pebbles in Carisbrook Well took a deeper dive in good esteem than he, when he set down the presumptuous nonsense about Thackeray's limitations, in the Morley series, as he did. He said, for instance, that Thackeray Was idle, and didn't know much about it, because he didn't write so many words an hour. Good Heavens! But certainly Thackeray was oddly defended by his friends, in some respects. I do not see why Shirley Brooks and others should have so resented his being called a cynic. Surely that is what he was, exactly ; and the greatest of all the cynics, on one side of his nature. Cynics are those who, out of their own hard experience, have ceased to believe in all the pleasant surfaces of life, and do not hold that when you have said " a good fellow," or "a charming woman," you have said everything. They scorn shams, but they know goodness when they see it, and do all they can to help it, and love it from their souls. Shirley Brooks seems to think Thackeray "wasn't a cynic, because he had a broad brow and blue eyes." But all cynics are not as ugly as Diogenes, living in their tubs instead of taking them. Thackeray's was the higher cynicism. He and his epitaph might have been written down in his own translation from the German lyric : for he was a poet as he was everything else, when the mood was on him:

Oh for all I have suffered and striven!
Care has embittered my cup and my feast:
But here is the night and the dark blue heaven,
And my soul shall be at rest.

Oh golden legends writ in the skies,
I turn towards you with longing soul,
And list to the awful harmonies Of
the spheres as on they roll.
My hair is grey and my sight nigh gone,
My sword it rusteth against the wall ;
Right have I spoken and right have I done;
When shall I rest me once for all ?

Oh blessed Rest! oh royal Night!
Wherefore seemeth the time so long,
Till I see yon stars in their fullest flight,
And list to their loudest song ?

CHAPTER IV

MY FATHER IN HIS HABIT AS HE LIVED

MY father must have had great qualities as a host, to gather round his table so many of the leading spirits of his day, both old and young. And all showed him an unfailing deference, except perhaps a wandering Buckle here and there. His force, as I knew him, did not so much lie in the readiness of speech attributed to him by Manning, as in the depth, variety, and accuracy of his knowledge. He talked little, but always well. And some of his fashions were very quaint. If he found himself next a neighbour to whom there was nothing to be said (for he had little or no small talk to spare) he relapsed into a courteous absence and occupied himself, perhaps, as he told me he once did when he was being photographed, in calculating how many ryots could cultivate a certain tract of land in India in a certain time. Next him was once a shy and quiet girl who was too frightened to speak, and he was only awakened to his own long silence by a general pause, as she was finishing a,very modest allowance of gooseberry tart Clearly and politely he said, " Have a glass of wine after all that pie ? " The poor girl looked as if she might have sunk into the earth. And I can remember his coming in at five one afternoon, when a new married young couple were paying my mother a ceremonial visit, with a bland smile on his face, his right hand stretched out and his left holding back the lappel of his frock-coat in one of his favourite attitudes, with the startling address in an insinuating voice, "Whom have we here?" Another time, when a harmless friend had been staying with us for a few days, and my mother announced that somebody else was coming instead, he said with a resigned sigh, " More mob?"

My father carried everything before him, in the old phrase, at Harrow and Oxford, where as commoner of Trinity, scholar of Oriel, and fellow of Balliol in succession, he was the first of the long and memorable line of Ireland scholars, Elden scholar and Professor of Political Economy. Like most of that stamp he joined the Bar, and at first supported himself by journalism on the Globe. Oddly enough the same paper might have laid the foundation of my own pen-and-ink work, as a mysterious overture was made to me soon after I had taken my degree, to write for it from private information on affairs of state. What might have become of me if I had consented has been often matter of speculation with me, but I was young and nervous and innocent of all political tendencies. Chamberlain's advice to politicians, to choose your party and stick to it through thick and thin (like the gentleman in Southey's "Terrible Journey from Moscow") might have made quite an important personage of me in the course of years. It was unlucky for my father that he chose Common Law instead of Chancery, as his was eminently the Chancery mind. He never could come down to a jury at all, and always saw the two sides of everything. At the Exeter sessions he held a brief in a case of which he felt the rights strongly, but could not make the Bench agree with him. In the next case he appeared, too, and simply re-marked : "In the last case I held a brief for the plaintiffs in which I was absolutely in the right, and you decided against me. Now I appear for the defendants. The facts are exactly similar and I am entirely in the wrong. So I must ask you to decide for me." And the Bench had to do it. Feeling himself on the wrong side of his profession, sound as was the repute he had in his way acquired, my father accepted the permanent secretaryship of the Colonies before he was forty. He gave up ambition for a certainty, though at a sacrifice of income at the first, arid became, as he said, " A dumb dog for the rest of his life." But he liked his quiet influence at the Colonial Office, and was interested in his work. When he took up the same post at the India Office he liked it less. It was in the latter days of John Company and Leadenhall Street, and then, as afterwards with the Indian Council, too many people wanted their own way. It was the old story of " too many cooks," he said. But his power of work was prodigious. He got up at comfortable hours, wrote for an hour or two in his study after breakfast, walked across the three parks to his office in the fine weather, got through all his business there generally by about four, played whist at a friend's or at the Athenaeum till dinner-time, and then walked home, and in the evening had his table in the drawing-room, and wrote articles for the *Edinburgh,* or leaders for the *Pall Mall* till he went to bed. This was in his later days, when, as he seemed to know everything about everything, nothing was any trouble. He rejoiced in his return to his early days of journalism, under the wing of good George Smith, most enterprising of publishers, more than in anything. His "little cheques" from the *P.M.G.* were a perpetual delight to him.

Out of his many side-tastes, he loved his whist the best, chiefly, I suppose, out of human perversity, because he couldn't play it. As he never had any delusions about himself he knew it quite well. An excited whist-player poured out to us once his interest in a lady he had met and described, who played the game, he thought, better than any woman he ever heard of. " She plays very often with an uncle of hers," he added, "who is always in the rubbers at the Athenaeum. And the best of it is," slapping his thigh with delight, " that she says he doesn't really understand it at all." " She is quite right," said my father mildly, "I am that uncle." He loved geology, and understood it, and was always discussing it with another of his friends, John Ball of Alpine fame, who was a brother secretary for the Colonies. Also he loved trees as much as Gladstone, and wandered about his Devonshire woods amongst them.

But instead of cutting them down with an axe, he marked them with a hatchet for the workmen to cut down. He was broad and strong, and an athlete in his younger days, but not in his elder. And his young imagination had given them all names, with the help of his brother Charles, the Roman historian and Dean of Ely. The " River Noitatnalp," otherwise Plantation backwards, ran through the woodlands of the grounds. And the wooden seats of indolence were Livias, and Cavadonga, and many names besides. I had to follow in the wake, and childlike called my own tree, Bal-a-bal-bal. And I found the name deep carven in the bark, not many years ago. And my favourite bit of wild wood I called the " Wildenforst," and my favourite aunt was my squire Rolf, and I the Baron Somebody, For I was of imagination all compact from childhood, and couldn't help it, with all its besetting dangers and all its incomparable charm. Joanna Baillie, poet and dramatist of **The Passions,** a quaint little figure propped on her Hampstead pillows, patted and felt my round child-head, and told my father I was bound to scribble, whether he liked it or not. And he did not like it, but I was so bound. If only I had not been obliged by well-meant parental pressure to devote so many years to becoming a bad lawyer, I might have been a good author, though who knows ? By the time I was ten I had written a five-act tragedy called **The Poisoned Pancake,** in which a vindictive cook poisoned the whole royal family and court at once, in the last act. It was like an early **Hamlet** The whole play, music, and entr'actes and all, might have been performed in ten minutes and a half. It is with curious pleasure that I learn that a very young and rather puritanic niece of mine has just embarked on a like experiment Heredity I suppose. Her father discovered a sample in her room, which ranthus:

ACT I.—SCENE 2.

KING EDWARD I. and COURTIERS discovered.

A COURTIER. My liege, a gentleman awaits below.
K. EDW. Oh, tell him to be d—-d. I want my lunch.

Likewise I had indited an additional book of Pope's Homer's **Iliad,** and jfchree supplementary canticles to the Psalms of David. My contemporary and ally, W. S. Gilbert, was wiser and more obstinate in his generation than I. He, too, was meant for the Bar. " If you would only stick to it," said his father, "you might become Lord Chancellor." "So I might," said W. S. "And if I stick to the theatres, I may become Sheridan. One's as likely as the other, and of the two I prefer Sheridan." And he did stick to them, and wasn't far wrong about the result There's nothing like sticking. Would that I had ever stuck. But it doesn't matter now. If I had made a fortune, my friend and " solicitor " would have stolen it all. "Sweet are the uses of variety." And I have enjoyed myself in my time, very much. These things are arranged for us by somebody. We do not arrange them on the broad lines.

My father's imagination made another start than mine. For by the time he was fourteen he had written a full and exhaustive criticism on "Gibbon's History," a work of which I have hinted my own sleepful awe. As to his forestry, he visited the States just after the Civil War. When he came back he wrote an article for ***Macmillan.*** Everybody expected something deep upon the situation. But it was all about the American trees, which he had been silently observing with the deepest closeness. Once, in his long connection with the ***Edinburgh,*** he was asked to write an article upon some abstruse subject, and did. There was much excitement, for he was accused of having pilfered it His article on the same subject had appeared in the same periodical in almost the same words many years before. And Henry Reeve was much exercised in mind. The earlier article proved to have been my father's own, and he had clean forgotten it. The same subject had suggested the same train of thought, that was all. For, like John Bright, he never changed his mind when it was once made up.

Another of his odd passions was heraldry. One of his games with me as a boy was `` bricks." The oblong bricks were knights, carefully painted with coats-of-arms in front, or horses which they sat on. The square bricks were heads, on pack-saddles. We played at " Ivanhoe," and the knights were Wilfred, and Front de Boeuf, and Ralph de Vipont And they sat in their tents, and we tilted with them. If a knight fell on his back he was wounded. If he fell on it three times running he was disabled. If he fell on his side he was dead. Once when my father was at the India Office, an order of a new "star" was created. The Prince Consort sent the design himself. It had four or six "points," I don't know which. The Heralds' Office was much excited, and my father endorsed their remonstrance. " The star," he pointed out, " never had four or six points." Prince Albert simply answered that it was time it had. When he left the Colonies for India, the Duke of Newcastle offered to make my father a K.C.B., and he said he didn't care about it. He had been a C.B. before. When he joined my mother at Nice, he casually told her of the offer. Womanlike and naturally, she was much distressed. So he wrote to the Duke and told him that to please his wife he should like to be a K.C.B. And the Duke was very sorry, but said that as the honours had now been given it was too late. And my father said thank you, but really it didn't matter. Unambitious in that, in literature, in everything. Instead of writing books himself, he was content to finish other men's books, if Longman or Murray asked him. In that way he finished the " Life of Francis " (Junius), and the " Life of Henry Lawrence." What he really was, was a philosopher of the most uncompromising kind. I have every material reason to wish that he had been less so. Yet he never wrote a book upon philosophy. But he had great strength, and was of large use. Sir George Bowen told me once that as long as my father was at the Colonial Office he never cared if he was right or wrong in a difficulty, for if he did his best he knew that he had " Merivale like a stone wall at his back." And so with many others. My father often discussed the vexed question of competitive examinations with me. Too much was made of it, he thought, but on the whole he believed in it The Anglo-Saxon, he said, has the same qualities always, and the governing quality is of all of them the first. If Clive had not been on the spot, some other, and very likely some more honest Clive would have been. Taken all things together, the man with the better brain will be the better man. Nobody would ever know, he added, except perhaps himself and those in his position, how often some difficulty on the frontiers, whether in India or the Colonies, brought us to the verge of a terrible war. Always there was some young Briton to the fore, to defy rule and assume authority at his own risk, and stay the mischief on his own responsibility. "While that quality lasts, we shall," my father said. And he made it his own rule, whatever the loud complaints at home, to stand steadily by the unruly subordinate, till all the facts were known, Yet he had every sympathy with the subject races, when to his mind oppression could be feared. He differed strongly from our famous cousin, Sir Battle

Frere, on many occasions, and he had no word of tolerance for Governor Eyre.

" I never knew," his cousin and successor at the India Office, Sir Lewis Mallet the Free-Trader told me, "what your father's power of work could be, until I followed him. I worked all day in his place, and sometimes more. Yet an assistant under-secretary and a legal adviser had to be both appointed, to help me through. He seemed to do thewhole of it without turning a hair." As he had been a lawyer, all the legal questions that arose were simply referred to him, and he decided them. The only duty which he confessed to me that he resented was being called upon to do what may be called the house-work. He did not like, when deep in some vital trouble in Madras or in Bombay, to be suddenly called upon to settle a private difference between the office housemaid and the office cook. He even thought that it might have been spared him, but took it like everything else, as it came. Not long ago I saw a wonderful and tiny actress, Louie Freear, a modern Mrs. Keeley in her way, play in a piece in which an enthusiastic audience made her sing a song about six times over. She was dressed as a drummer, and two big soldiers set her on a table to do it The last time she looked at the biggest of them, and said quietly to him instead of the audience, " Well, you do want a lot for your money, you do." And perversely I thought of my father, and of the British Government.

At odd hours he could poetise with the best of us. None of his verses have been published, I think, save a few here and there. Let me finish this chapter with one example, founded upon an old monkish piece of doggerel, and written for his baby son:

Fide Deo. Die sæpe preces. Peccare caveto.
Sis humilis. Pacem dilige. Magna fuge.
Multa audi. Dic pauca. Tace secreta.Minori
Parcito. Majoricedito. Ferto parem.
Propria fac. Ne differ opus. Sis æquus ecquc
Serva pacta. Pati disce. Memento mori

Since, my child, as now we sever,
Thou and I full oft must part,

I would fain be present ever
In thine heart.

Golden words and precepts leaving
As a father's gifts for thee.
With thy holiest thoughts enweaving
Thoughts of me.

Thou art yet too young for learning,
All untamed thine infant-will,
Scarce with feeble glance discerning
Good from ill.
Yet I deem, if rightly reading
All that open brow should speak,
And the smile so gravely spreading
O'er thy cheek.

Thou wilt one day learn and treasure,
As thou should'st, this Latin rhyme,
 Words uncouth and homeliest measure,
Thoughts sublime.

Put thy trust in Him who made thee,
Feel the presence of His eye,
Ever, when life's ills invade thee
Then most nigh.
He has taught to erring mortals
To His palace-gate the way;
Prayer can reach those distant portals.
Learn to pray.

But, since empty prayers avail not
Heaven's eternal crown to win,

Watching still, and striving, fail not;
Flee from sin.

Be thou humble; 'tis His teaching,
Who the proudest can o'erthrow;
Yet still list the fond beseeching
Of the low.

Follow Peace, and so ensue her;
Fortune, with her changeful brow,
Let the world's gay children woo her,
Woo not thou.

Swift to hear, and slow to utter,
Others' wisdom make thine owll;
What thy friends in secret mutter
Tell to none.

With the weaker be forbearing;
With the stronger courteous be;
With thine equal be thy bearing
Kind and free.

Do the work thy fortunes shape thee,
Wheresoe'er thy lot be cast;
Seize the hours that fain would 'scape thee,
Gliding past.

See the poor and feeble righted,
Shield him from the man of strife;
Keep the word thou once hast plighted
As thy life.

Learn to suffer; 'tis a training
Time must teach the roughest breast;
But the mild and uncomplaining
Use it best.

Last, that thou may'st smile unshrinking
When the long dark hour draws nigh,
When life's wearied pulse is sinking,
Learn to die.

CHAPTER V

MY UNCLES

NOT proposing ever to be an old fogey if I can help it—for though I don't see why a fogey should fail to be acceptable, I should like to escape the imputation—I desire not to laudate the ***acta tempora*** at the expense of the present In many ways Mat Arnold's "stream of tendency that makes for righteousness " makes likewise for improvement, and in some ways the world is better than it was in the days when Plancus was my consul. In others perhaps it is not. There are a good many, by-the-bye, to whom such a phrase may be in itself fogeyesque. Have I not twice cited Latin in six lines ? My excuse for them is that they are very old quotations. But that to which I fain would lead is this. I must think and maintain that respect for elders in a younger generation is at once a MY UNCLES Stouching and a refining thing, and that it is going out of fashion. I never liked to aim at the hail-fellow well-met with my distinct seniors, as too many of the younger men do now. I liked to preserve the " Mr." even when on terms most intimate, and I cannot help missing its use towards myself, save at my own desire. The slang word " form " is always being used at this present, and not too often followed. The change in this matter, though in my eyes new, is nothing of the kind, of course. Nothing is. Like the Arnoldian tendency, all is gradual. It was before my day that sweet Charles Lamb— why is it that an epithet, generally affected and objectionable, applieth always with such a pleasant charm to him ?—discoursed on courtesy's decay in his essay on "Modern Gallantry." It has been sliding ever since.

So I will again expose myself to the old penalty of a sconce—or fine for quoting Latin, which nowadays would not mount up to much—and say " ***Heu pietas ! hen prisca fides! " Which means that, like a reverent youth once more, in right of my moment's subject-matter, I turn from my father to discourse about my uncle, before inflicting my more personal self. For they were nearly of an age, and distinguished scholars in their day. Both were at Harrow. My father was at Oxford. My uncle was at Cambridge, and connected with the famous Tennyson-Hallam-Monckton-Milnes set of the apostles. Briton-like, the distinction he most valued to the last was having been one of the crew in the first Oxford and Cambridge race. Next, I think, he was apt to pride himself upon his indifference to Greek. "What a splendid scholar you would be, Merivale," said his witty friend, Thompson, afterwards master of Trinity, " if you knew any Greek at all." Nevertheless he did translate the*** Iliad. But in Latin my uncle was the first past-master of his day, and by degrees his subject led him to his position as one of the best-known of Roman historians, unpleasing to the school of Freeman, but finished and admirable in his own. " I wish you would bring out a book about somebody newer," I wrote to him irreverently one day. For he was a genuine humorist and a first-rate letter writer. "My dear boy, was his answer, "certainly not If you only knew the comfort of con-fining yourself to historical assertions, about a people who are dead and gone and can't contradict you!" I quarrelled with him for keeping out of his books the humour which ran over in his talk and letters. But in those days at all events, to write as you talk was wrong. Look at the novels and plays of the time, and measure Thackeray's value as taking us back to the tongues understood of men. Nobody who didn't know him would have accused the Roman historian of being a humorist, but he had the good old college conviction that you must be deep or nothing. Nothing lies so deep as humour, but there are many who never see that If you are not heavy and hard of reading, you are only frivolous. In the quaint old library of the deanery, he took up the Lives of the Judges, or some such deservkig-well-ofi-foeaven labour, and asked me why, oh why, I didn't do some work like that! " So

I would, uncle," I answered with scant reverence, "if I couldn't do anything of my own." S had just brought out some foolish play or another, and answered without reflecting. ' But my uncle chuckled for ten minutes.

He was of course a great authority in the schools at both Universities, and nearly led me into a scrape when I was at Balliol. It was the custom there to write an English essay every week. Half of the men read their essays to the Master, the other to their college tutors. And it was a bad habit of ours, I'm afraid, to let one do duty for two sometimes, by lending our works to a friend who read in the other quarter from ourselves. Having an essay on some Rompn subject to write, I founded it upon my uncle's history, and read it to the Master. And I lent it to another man, who read it to his tutor. And his tutor said: " Ah, Mr. -—, I see that you have followed Merivale very closely." Well, he had. But he was a man of cool and ready wit, and placidly replied: " Yes sir, I have. I thought Mr. Merivale's history quite the safest authority." "Quite right, Mr. -— You couldn't have done better. That friend of mine is now a judge, grave, and of the highest rank, I wonder if he remembers it. He was something of a scapegrace, under—even then—his learned man-ner, and used to lead that same tutor a life. For the tutor was a character, quaint, fidgety, and very particular about routines. My friend's rooms were over his head, and it so happened that one morning I made one of a breakfast-party at my friend's. It was a decidedly cheerful party, and ended in a general encounter in our shirt-sleeves, with dumb-bells and boxing-gloves, or chairs for those who had them not. And in the midst of the revelry there was a stroke upon the oak, and the tutor's scout came in. " Gentlemen," he said, " the Dean of Chapel" (which was the tutorial rank) " wishes me to say that he cannot overlook this disturbance " (for he was a very dour scout) "and is himself coming to speak with you at once." " Beg him to come up," said our host respectfully. " Certainly, sir." And the scout retiring, we stood aghast But my friend was equal to the occasion. "Where's my prayer-book?" he said. I was puzzled. Was he going to say his prayers to the offended Dean, or what? "I thought so," he went on, after looking down the introductory pages. " It's all right" And the Dean came in, fussy and fuming, like an angry turkey-cock. And he spake in his wrath, and talked of gates and other penalties. When the first burst was over, mine host gave his explanation calmly: " Sir, it is now half-past eleven o'clock. It is a Saint's day, and we made sure that you were at University Sermon." Detected in his own sins, the Dean became fussily apologetic, as he always did when taken off his guard " Well, Mr. — I did intend to go. Of course I intended to go. But other occupations intervened, and you see that—if you didn't know I was at home it is of course quite another thing, and I'm quite sorry if I interrupted your enjoyment" " Don't mention it, sir," said our host blandly. And the incident ended in forgiveness all round. Well I remember that young man a few years later, when we were both reading for the Bar in town, going with me and another to the boxing-rooms of a famous professional light-weight who proposed to give us lessons. Professing an ignorance of the art, he declined at first, but the champion prevailed on him to try, gave him a pair of dumb-bells to help him to hit out with, and then told him to hit out at him. And so he did. He was small and strong and wiry, and proceeded to brandish the instruments close to the professional head, in such fashion that to land one would probably have been fatal— following it all round the room in a kind of Pyrrhic dance. The dodging and manoeuvres of the bruiser were beautiful to see. He had enough of it first, and only closed the encounter by earnest remonstrance, the two spectators laughing till they couldn't speak.

My uncle always credited Dr. Thompson with the best classical pun he remembered. In his common-room days one of the fellows bore the name of Money. But he took to himself a wife and retired, and grew noted for his uxorious ways. On the lady becoming as one of those who love their lords, somebody said of Money that the nearer the event approached, the more marked his devotion became. " Quite so," said Thompson. "Crescit amor nummi, quantum ipsa pecunia crescit." The delicate difference of gender could scarcely be more wittily marked. In later days it fell to my own lot to know he Master of Trinity and appreciate him. It was during a summer course at Kissingen, where waters were being taken. I was always a good companion for an elder of that mark, to be taken a walk with, for it was a delight to me to listen and to learn. He made many a stroll pleasant for me in that way, with the dry, observant humour that was always on the alert. He dressed carelessly, seedily even, and was discoursing about the superior ease and freedom of foreign manners when we passed a hand-some, furred, distinguished-looking man elaborately dressed, who saluted the Master in passing with a courteous freedom.

" Just what I was saying," Dr. Thompson remarked when he was gone. " You and I couldn't have done it like that. Superiority without patronage. So thoroughly affable." "What is he?" I said; "a Russian nobleman?" " No ; he's my courier."In that same pleasant character of humorist my uncle was more at home than many who get more common credit for it. It was at the bottom of his whole character, I think, as it was under that of Dr. Vaughan, of Harrow, but I suppose that neither of them showed it much to the outside world. When Gladstone bestowed the Deanery of Ely upon him he was surprised as well as thankful, as nobody denounced that great man and all his works more strenuously than he. But the only result was a pleasant conviction that the Minister's magnanimity rose from his never having heard of him. Was he the last of the old school of Deans ? 1 think so. It was a pleasant school, and the idea of it was graceful. The honourable and quiet retreat for the retired and well-graced scholar, away from the boom to look after his cathedral and his services, to enrich the world from his study with appropriate work, and grow old in leisured dignity, was rather a pleasant thing of rest apart, in a world that wants so much to do something active, whether it has it to do or not. The duties of a dean are by their constitution but of a passive kind. So the new school make some for themselves and collide with their bishops much accordingly. Never interfering with his bishops, and never interfered with by them, he said that they found him a model in all ways, though I grieve to say that even Sydney Smith himself hardly made more fun than he did amongst intimates, and in his quiet way, of the perplexities of an excellent set of men who now, even more than in his time, are obliged to wear as many different colours as Joseph's coat in order to suit everybody. His own view of Ritualism was simple; namely, that it was foolish but harmless, and that if people liked that sort of thing, there was no reason why they shouldn't. He didn't, and there was no reason why he should. But as his character had depth as well as breadth, he would have been of great value to church-schism now. Things in his letters lately published show singular fore-knowledge of our time. But deaneries were still retreats for thinkers then. And when my father wrote to congratulate him on his appointment as exactly the right thing, he answered that everybody seemed to think so. " All my Cambridge friends," he said, "are writing to offer me beds, under the evident impression that for the rest of my life I've only to go to sleep." My father and uncle were faithful friends and allies always, though, thanks to our old acquaintances known as Circumstances over Which &c., they met but very seldom in the later days. They were of an age within the year, but no temperaments could have been much more different, except in their curious indifference to the successes of the world. Of my father's characteristics I have spoken, and of his old Palmerstonian Liberalism, tempered by his convictions of the danger as well as the greatness of the English governing qualities. His very strong sympathy for the oppressed everywhere led him into unpopular times more than once, where native races or the rights of the weaker were concerned. My uncle's knowledge of his beloved Roman world was absolute and exhaustive. For the rest he was content with such learning as men of his intellect cannot fail to acquire. And he always used to regret in his amusing way to my father that his own example of knowing one thing and sticking to it had not been followed by his elder. His own political views were the simplest and highest old Tory; and my father's scruples about natives he confessed to be quite beyond him. " It's all very well," he said; " but if these good people talk about washing their spears in my blood, all I know is that I prefer to wash mine in theirs." So he was quite in sympathy with his wife's kinsman, Sir Battle Frere, the strongly mild South African Proconsul, with the iron hand in the velvet glove, whose name seems to have slipped out of the record just when it should be remembered most So high was the position he took up about the wars that preluded the great event, so firm his protests against the policy of Half-a-Heart which has caused such mischief and vacillation, so clear his view of the danger of alienating the then friendly Boers, that his advice would have preserved us from the need of the endless war of supremacy which the Policy of the Half-Heart made by degrees inevitable. He was cruelly treated by the Half-Heart himself, as so often has been the lot of faithful servants who cannot change their minds abroad when Government changes sides at home. It was the old story of the neutral shuttlecock between the party battledores. They keep it going as long as they can use it against each other, and then drop it between them. I am free to confess that, young as I was, my sympathies were with my uncle, and not my father, there. In wars of supremacy I scarcely see where questions of metaphysical right and wrong come in. For it is those wars that have made history, geography, and everything else that is human. And till the human note has been transposed uncounted octaves, I see not whence the change in them is to come.

One day upon the sands at Cromer my father was walking with Vice-Chancellor Wickens, a man, like himself, of very wide reading. Behind them followed dear go-ahead Tom Brown Hughes, of fame undying as long as school-boys shall be athletic—the last distinction that just now they seem likely to lose—and myself. He stopped short suddenly, and pointed to the two backs before him. "There," he said, "goes the entire sum of human knowledge. There is nothing upon earth that one of those two men doesn't know." My uncle, with all his humorous way, had an unbounded reverence for my father's knowledge. They corresponded always and on all things on public questions and on all beside, and I remember well how once the Dean wrote triumphantly to the other, to point out how on some Roman argument he had demolished Niebuhr. My father rather agreed, and thought he had. But placidly added that Niebtthr's was a name recognised as strong as theirs, and that the world would very soon forget that Niebtthr had been demolished. Very much what Sir George Bowen said to me of the loss, my uncle said after my father died. It was not only the brother, and friend, and correspondent who was gone before, but the rock of advice and judgment He said that on all the points on which he was wont to consult his elder as soon as occasion arose, he felt like one lost at sea. They were certainly a strong par fratrum, who might have been most things if they had only cared. Looking at a tablet-roll in Balliol Hall the other day of her more honoured and distinguished sons, I missed my father's name, though that of the first Ireland scholar, Professor of Political Economy, and much besides. Amongst great names and fussy mediocrities, I found him not. In ignorant awe I wondered who was Purvis, and where was Swinburne. I suppose that modern Balliol never heard of him, in her classic shades. Yet " Atalanta in Calydon" is not unclassical. Modesty is a great mistake. I'm all for Purvis ; greatness is the Don's.

My own chief link with my uncle, always, was our common sense of fun. With me he was always at his most amusing, which was delightful. It was beyond him to resist a joke. An enterprising firm of publishers of the day, guiltless of much discrimination, asked Anthony Trollope for a life of Julius Caesar, as part of a series. As a popular novelist he was good enough for them, though scholarship was not, perhaps, his strong point He produced it at once, as he would produce anything asked for, at so many words an hour, which by his own account was his method, to be ensued, he thought, by every author. He was much exercised in mind about Thackeray's lack of industry, as he said in his memoir, because there were so many hours when Thackeray wrote no words at all. They were not bad when they came, perhaps, on the whole These publishers, no doubt, thought that the best man to deal with Julius Cæsar, at this hour of the day, would be a writer of romance. Proud of his achieveme nt in so new a line, Trollope, an old friend of our family, at once sent a copy to my uncle, the Dean, who replied with placid brevity : "Thank you for your Comic History of Caesar. Trollope wept But Trollope's chief friend in our race was another uncle of another kind, known to his many friends as Johnnie. He was a junior brother, who never did anything he could avoid. And in that way he avoided a good deal. He was supposed to be like my father; and, as both were well known in London, though in quite different sets, he used often to see the dawn of recognition in a stranger's face in the ways. So he would go up to him at once with, "You think I'm my brother. I'm not. Good morning." Much pleased at first when Trollope sent him all his novels as they came out, he began at last gravely to medi-tate how to build a new room. He re-joiced in my producing plays, declaring that Themis and Thespis were a fine pair to drive, and wrote, " I hear you have written a play for Wiggins. Good. He was a good actor, for I knew him once. I remember Mrs. Wiggins as Miss Jones—a sorry jade at best. Don't repeat that to Wiggins. Managers are a thin-skinned race." He was an odd fish, Johnnie. Taking a house in the suburbs with a garden, like so many other true cockneys, he didn't know what to do with it A country chum came to show him, and walked him up and down. " Now look at these. You have a fine crop of these. First you must do so-and-so in July, then such-and-such in September, and next year there will be something to remember.0 "Quite so," said my uncle, when he had quite finished. " But I must begin at the beginning. In the first place what are these ? " " " Good Lord! Potatoes." I think that Uncle John kept the worst wine I ever drank, on the whole, if he could be said to keep it For he would buy a bottle of anything he fancied at a public on his way home to dinner, and carry it in his coat-pocket At one of his cheery men-dinners we had a pompous guest, almost a stranger, who addressed his host at once as " Johnnie/' like all the rest But the host didn't care for liberties, in his way; and when the stranger began to praise his wine, he twinkled. And we all knew something was coming. " Ah! I see you really do understand about wine. These fellows don't You're worth it; so after dinner I'll give you a glass you will remember." And he gave secret instructions to his maid-servant, who at the proper time brought a bottle with due care. With care it was opened and dusted at the mouth, and a glass poured out especially for the guest " Now, tell me what you think of that" The guest sipped it, rolled it round with his tongue, held it up to the lamp and winked one eye at it, and went through all the Maskelyne and Cookery of the conscious expert upon these occasions. " Splendid, Johnnie! really splendid!" "I knew you'd think so, I saw you were a judge." " Well" (modestly) " I ought to be. Now, Johnnie, how long have you had that in your cellars ?" " Exactly three-quarters of an hour." The maid had been sent out to buy it, round the corner. In youth he was an oddity to the finger-tips, and it was he, though the story has been appropriated for more than one more famous wit, who, when as a hard-up undergraduate he was called upon by a collector for the conversion of the Jews, politely regretted his inability, but added as he bowed out his visitor, " Look here. If you like to send me a Jew, I'll try to convert him." I take this opportunity, at chestnut-hazard, to claim his own for him. When in his early London days afterwards his brother Charles came from Cambridge for a few days, he informed his family that he had never once seen John, because at whatever hour of the day he called, John was always out at breakfast.

CHAPTER VI

MY PEDIGREE

MY father, lover of pedigrees, always held that with but a break or two he could trace the descent from Andrew Marvel. For ours is an odd name, with no English counterpart. As Mervayle first it appeared in the old Elizabethan register, the first to be found in the records of the North-amptonshire hamlet of Middleton-Chaney, and from father to son a succession of sturdy Puritan yeomen cultivated each his own field, with no ambition to enlarge the boundaries. Forty-six entries of the name stand in the register between 1558 and 1770; and a tradition amongst us that the line began at Middleton Cheney in 1590 with William Merivale, a fugitive from persecution in France, was dispelled by my father's examination on the spot, in that same year of fifty-one which opened my veracious narrative. As the highest mortuary fee was paid for William Merivale, he must have been a man of warmth in his day ; and the first spelling of Mervayle suggests an undoubted French origin in Merveille or Merville, the French equivalent of the English Seaton. The first rude forefather of the hamlet I can fix was Henry Mervayle, son of John Mervayle and Margaret his wife, baptized into an equally rude world on October 21, 1558, And in 1860 Thomas Merivale, head of the family and owner of four or five cottages in the lower village, dwelt still in Middleton-Chahey as the father of four sons and two daughters. Evidently, as a cheery Norwegian parent of twenty-four observed to me amongst his fjords, my elder branch still does its best to increase the popularity.

My own and younger branch began in 1667 with the birth of a cadet, John Merivale, who left his village on the elder coming into the small family property, and started in life as a stocking-weaver at Northampton. He must have been a constituent of the Labouchere of his day, and probably voted for him. Marrying Hannah Moore, the daughter of a Baptist minister, he became the father of a curious and interesting character, in the shape of—to give him his full honour in that respect—my great-great-grandfather, Samuel Merivale, who migrated to Tavistock and grafted us on the Devonian stock, in the character of a Dissenting minister. We seem to have been the most uncompromising Nonconformists ; and at my hours I feel the strain still in my blood, refusing, indeed, still in heart to conform to praying for the wisdom and understanding of all the Lords at all seasons, and of all the Commons only whilst sitting, at stated times and in whatever mood. Samuel himself had something of the rebellious streak, however, for in place of Baptist he turned Presbyterian, and abjured the errors of Calvin for the rival ones of Arminius. But it was no slight thing for a Presbyter to be ordained in those days, and Samuel, who was a capital letter-writer, describes the function thus : " The entire solemnity was managed with great gravity and decency, and my heart was warmed, and my mind, I hope, seriously impressed with the transaction I was engaged in. Mr. Cranch, of Modbury, a gentleman of great worth and ingenuity, one of my particular acquaintance, began a short prayer, and read a psalm and chapter. Then they sang a hymn. Mr. Walters, of Chudleigh, a man of no great note but of some considerable standing in the ministry, then prayed for about half an hour. Afterwards Mr. Moore, of Plymouth, the most learned minister in this country, and a man of equal modera-tion and candour, gave us a most excellent sermon of more than an hour, on the office and duties of a Christian bishop. Mr. Baron, of Plymouth, as being the oldest minister present, then went into the pulpit; and after a short account of the nature and design of ordination, demanded for the satisfaction of all present an account of my faith, which I then delivered, standing in a seat facing the pulpit. At first I had a pretty tremour upon me, which by degrees wore off, and I spoke with courage, so as to be very well heard by all. Then nine questions were proposed to me each of which I answered distinctly. After this, Mr. Baron came down into the seat where I was, and in a very solemn manner recommended me to God by prayer, and set me apart for the pastoral office. After this they sang again. Mr. Brett, of Liskeard, a man of great oddity in his appearance and behaviour, but of much inward worth and ex-cellence, gave the charge in a plain, honest, familiar way, which consisted of several useful directions relating to my conduct as a Christian, a minister, and a Protestant dissenter. Then they sang a third tune, and Mr. Wills, of Appledore, concluded with a prayer." As I read through this programme now, I feel a certain pride in thinking that it appears to have taxed all the resources of Devonshire, and some of Cornwall, to ordain my great great-grandfather. They did take their turns in those days, they did; but some of the turns on the platform must have been a thought too long. When Mr. Wills, of Appledore, was called on, I suspect that there were dark thoughts about. Modbury and Appledore must have seemed unto the assembly even as another Dan and Beersheba. After this they sang again. I like my ancestor for his pretty tremour. Somehow, forty-five pounds a year, however, for the Presbyterian cure of Tavistock, seems but a modest stipend after all that pie.

Samuel went the way of the world and fell in love with Jane Shellaber, a lady who " though no beauty, had many charms, which by degrees found their way to his heart." She died, however, and he transferred his affections to her sister Betsy, corresponding with her as Charissa under the name of Fidelio. His proposal by let-ter was as then proposals should be : " Should you rob me at Once," he wrote, "of all those pleasing hopes I have entertained, though I could have no reason to complain of your Injustice, yet give me leave to say it would give me such a shock as I know not how I could support But if, on the other hand, your Compassion, Generosity, and Tenderness prevail, I shall esteem myself the happiest of men, and shall make it the whole Business of my life to con vince you with what Sincerity, Gratitude, and Affection I am, dearest Madam, Your Lover, Friend, and Servant, S. MERIVALE."

All these substantives with the big initials prevailed in time, and they were married and did well, the sudden death of an intestate cousin who owned the estate of Annery near Bideford, famous through " Westward Ho," bringing the couple an accession of something like a small fortune for their share. In other ways, too, Samuel did well, in that his neighbours feasted him at Christmas, in one instance at"a very elegant entertainment off a leg of Mutton boiled, a Turkey very nicely roasted, a cheek of Pork, delicate minced Pyes, an Apple Pye and Gloucestershire Cheese, several sorts of Pickles, and variety of other Sauce. After Dinner there was Brandy and Rum and three sorts of Wine, and a noble Bowie of Arrack Punch. At Tea there was some of the richest Sweetmeat Cake ever tasted." Samuel's sermon the next morning is not on record.

But Charissa died .and Fidelio married again, this time an early love, wedded and widowed betweenwhiles, and left at his death one surviving son John, who at nineteen had engaged himself to a Fraulein from Exeter, Ann Katenkamp, aged seventeen, whose grandfather was a Calvinist minister at Bremen. Among his friends was Baring of Mount Radford in Exeter, the father of Sir Francis Baring, and upon the death of the Bremen minister, his son, Herman Katen-kamp, came over to Exeter and entered the Baring counting-house, Ann Katenkamp grew up a bright and cultivated girl, though, according to one of her brothers, she was "a very bad poet, who he hoped would never attempt to write verses again." The Herman and the bad poetry have stuck ever since. And John, the husband of Ann Katenkamp, begat as his elder child John Herman, who married the daughter of Dr. Drury, of Cock-wood, Devon, the famous scholar and head-master of Harrow. And likewise a younger daughter Fanny, who became the wife of John Lewis Mallet, son of Mallet du Pan, a distinguished French journalist and publicist, who took refuge in England with the rest of the king's adherents during the revolutionary times. And one of their sons became Sir Lewis Mallet, my father's cousin and successor in his India

Office post, and the foremost ally of Bright and Cobden in the early battles of Free Trade. And John, husband of Ann Katcnkamp, sold Annery and bought Barton Place by Exeter, formerly called Cowley Barton, the family-place which, with the rest of the lumber, has passed away from me, for the life of me I know not why, having as far as in me lies but striven to do my best for all men. But I wore my early and mature life out in trying to keep the peace at home, and I sate among scribes and players instead of on the woolsack, and crowned it all with the unpardonable sin. I lost my money.

Nay, but I have a motto which my forefathers had not I wonder what those forefathers, surveying their hapless descendant, think about it all. "Valeat Merendo," let him prosper by deserving. If that be the way to prosper, it is but poorly fitted to the race just now. Nor know I who invented that strange pun and took it out with arms when I was ill. It was without knowledge or consent of mine, head, as I avow, of my blue-blooded and warm-hearted clan. We had an odd crest in my father's time, a pollard crest without a tail attached, bearing some strange resemblance to the head of a Stag. At is still on my hereditary ink-bottles, and is the only hereditary thing that has not been taken away from me. My hereditary library, like my hereditary home, was most of it sold by somebody for somebody else's benefit likewise when I was ill. I have not cared even to try to trace it All that I could do was to stick my new arms and motto —somebody having bought them for me— upon my envelopes. But it is a practice that I drop. They made me laugh at first. They irritate me now. And we of the yeoman blood have got no earthly right to them,

Upon the mother's side it's quite another thing. There I defy inspection and rejoice in scutcheons and am blue, springing from the highest of the high, the county families. Archbishop Laud was my direct ancestor and inaugurated persecution. In the form of Christian name he still survives amongst us. From the sporting point of view of stock, Archbishop Laud and Andrew Marvel between them should be good enough for anybody. The first Robinson baronet—for we are thus red-handed, and from an odd coincidence they, too, were of Northampton-shire—was Lord Mayor of London in the days of loose King Charles. He had to do with the fire, or the plague, or something. And I grieve much to say that Pepys himself speaks of the first Lady Robinson as a monstrous fine woman no better than she should be. I wonder if any Stuart corpuscles got into the very allopathic blend which appears to have produced me. The Robinsons have bravely gone on unto the present day, though with no special gifts I know of except for violent quarrel amongst themselves in good old county-family fashion. But county blood within the veins hath yet its uses. In Rome I found myself once at dinner at my hostelry, next a Northamptonshire mother and daughter of that current They thought but little of me on my own account until they found out my maternal claim. Then I was as one of themselves and intimate. The youthful daughter opened like a flower, and assured me in county confidence that she was in love with Rome, especially the new parts,

CHAPTER VII

LITERARY AND THEATRICAL BEGINNINGS

WE had a right to our literary weaknesses between us, for my grandfather, John Herman, was a Commissioner in Bankruptcy in the flesh—was a poet and dramatist and man of letters in the spirit He was a close friend of Lord Byron, and wrote an epic of no mean mark in its day on the romantic story of " Orlando in Roncesvalles," in the metre of his great ally's " Don Juan," full of the old strain of chivalry which has but an archaic interest now, and for but few of us. I still like to read at times myself about those amorous and fearless Paladins, and the high-mettled Christian maidens of a kindred mould to theirs :

Hope lives through fear; who saith that hope is vain ?
Worm of the earth! canst thou presume to trace
The eternal limits of God's holy reign,
Infinite justice and unfailing grace ?

Will heaven destroy its own fair work again ?
Or, after some dark, doubtful, lingering space,

All with one voice eternal truth adore,
And humbly sue for peace and gain what they implore?

Beyond the pillars of this world of old,
Far o'er yon western flood's unmeasured plain,
Of other worlds the spirit darkly told,
For ages lost, for ages to remain
Unvisited by light divine, and cold
As Zembla's rocks which endless frosts enchain;
Yet hath the sun of Grace, to them unknown,
E'en for those cheerless realms and untaught nations shone.

But it was as a translator that my grandfather was at his best, and his versions of Schiller's "Diver" and "Song of the Bell" have all the ring of the originals. The first Lord Lytton's translation of the former scarcely approached its older rival. My grandfather's essays in play-writing—for I certainly can plead atavism for my own sins, the Galton form of heredity which skips a generation like rheumatic gout— began in an interesting fashion. His wife's father—Devonian like himself—was the famous scholar and head-master, Dr. Drury; and both loved the play. And, on a fit-up stage in Exeter, one night they saw a strolling player enact Othello and Harlequin. And so overcome and startled were they by the man's extraordinary power, that my grandfather at once wrote to Byron, then of the managing committee of Drury Lane which was but at a low ebb, and advised him to find the player out. Byron only laughed and pooh-poohed him, assuring him that he was always hearing of these wandering genii, who never came to anything. But Drury Lane ebbed more and more, and one morning my grandfather got a letter from him to say that something had to be done, and that if the Exeter genius could be unearthed he would give him a, chance on the recommendation of so good a critic. So the seekers set to work, and after much ado discovered the wanderer in some out-of-the-way corner of mere rustic Devon, ebbing like Drury Lane, and run low down indeed The story that followed is known to all the world, for the poor world-tossed genius went to London, and waited hopelessly enough for the chance that came at last And they called him at the theatre " the little man in the capes," and his name was Edmund Kean perhaps he was the greatest actor, if we may trust all the records, who ever flashed upon our stage. And it was not only as Shy lock that he appeared. In a metaphorical sense he repeated his Exeter experiment " They say that the fellow is a good Harlequin," said an envious member of the company, after he had struck the empty benches into fire, till "no one could have thought that so few people could kick up such a row." " Yes," said the kindlier Fawcett " He's the best I ever saw. For he has jumped at once over all our heads together." The next thing that my grandfather did was to write for the little-great man. I have just taken down from my book-shelves " Richard Duke of York, or the Contention of York and Lancaster, as altered from Shakespeare's three parts of Henry VI. In five acts, as it is performed at the Theatre Royal, Drury Lane, 1817." It strikes me as very ably done, after the Cibberian fashion of Shakespearean arrangement. Appropriate passages from Hey wood's " Royal King and Loyal Subject," or Chapman's " Byron's Conspiracy," are introduced to fill the spaces in the story, and some comic talk for Jack Cade and his followers is "borrowed from a very loyal play founded by Croune (who was a court poet in the reign of Charles II) on Shakespeare's Henry VI., and entitled *The Misery of Civil War,* 4to, 1680." Such passages as the compiler supplied himself for his plot's necessities make no immodest invasion of Shakespearean regions, but are both sound and apposite, as in a little scene just before the close, between York and his son Rutland.

> YORK. Cease, my good lords—my sons, Edward and Richard,
> On the Welsh marches, but abide my summons,
> With valiant Warwick for their sure defence.
> Should it go ill with me, oh ! bid them save
> Their lives and fortunes for a happier day
> I Bring in my dear boy Rutland.
>
> *Enter* RUTLAND *with a Priest, his tutor,*
> My darling ! Let me kiss thee ere I go.
> I know not if I e'er shall see thee more.
> If I should fall I leave thee to thy brothers,
> All valiant men ; and I will charge them all,

On my last blessing, to take care of thee
As of their souls.

RUTL. Why do you talk thus, father ?
If you must die I hope I shall die with you—
I'd rather die with you than live a king!
YORK. Sweet boy I Farewell, my soul I—Here, take the child,
And guard him safely in the donjon Tower.
Should things go ill, bear him away betimes,
And give his brothers notice of your flight

One of the author's supposed hereditary foes, the critics, severely reprehended my grandfather for modernising Shakespeare, and by way of contrast and reproof quoted the above, as his own "favourite passage in the original." Even so, when once I brought out a comedy intended as a faint Reflection of Faust, in modern life, and for my devil pictured a cynical wit and adventurer amongst a mob of foolish people, one of the same, and rather eminent, informed his readers that " Mr. Merivale was sometimes witty, but often puerile." Well, just what I had tried to be. That a dramatist should speak through his characters had not occurred to him. Another rebuked me gravely for carrying my parable so far, as to introduce " Mephistopheles's poodle " in the guise of the adventurer's servant. Which only means that, in Goethe's poem, Mephis-topheles himself is first brought into Faust's study in the guise of a poodle. Not that I am one of those who are the least disposed to quarrel with hard work like a critic s, having indeed been largely always one of them myself. But I wish they would make more sure before so committing themselves, some-times. A little learning is a dangerous thing. Have a long drink, or let it alone and have done with it

Like Lamb, I love a play-bill And I like to learn from the front page of this same " Richard, Duke of York," that the cast held such actors, besides Kean himself, as Pope, Holland, and Powell; Wallack and T. P. Cooke, of **Black-Eyed Susan** fame (whom in his old age I once must have beheld), Knight, Munden, Oxberry, and Mrs. Glover. In the preface, which it was then the fashion to supply to the published play, my grandfather speaks of the acting of the last famous lady, in the character of Queen Margaret, as a triumph of tragic power and feeling— a curious prelude to the

Mrs. Malaprop of the later days whom I can myself recall. As I have written in some other place, a youth of tragedy is a fine training for a ripe age of the more masterful comedy. Of Edmund himself my grandfather said that the character of York was absolute in his own creation; in Shakespeare, as we all know, hardly tangible. It had a good life in its day—the play—and led to Byron's begging my grandfather to write for him regularly, and to give him above all a comedy. But no more blank verse, an he loved him. " A good pantomime," wrote the author of Man-/red and Sardana-palus, " pays better than fifty Shakespeares." That letter of Byron's came into my possession, and, when I remember the author, has always amused me much. But my grandfather was far too tangled in the highly respectable—where even passably honest—mazes of the law, to be free to indulge his tastes as author or as playwright as freely as his more rebellious grandson. Ye gods! the number of the finer brains and spirits of which that pretentious calling has robbed a martyred world!

Lord Westbury, in one hour's talk with me one day, taught me more law than all the pleaders and conveyancers whom to my sorrow I have known. He said that I was logical of mind, and bade me hold by it, and cultivate clearness of expression. " Logic well put," he said, " take it all round, is apt to make the good law, and confound the bad. Your advisers, to begin with, will always be telling you what to do. Don't listen to it, but tell them. Tell them at once not to begin by puzzling their brains to find out the law against you. That's neither their affair nor yours, but the court's. Judges and Bar are right enough, on the whole, when you can get at them. Find out your strong points for yourself, and tell the men to stick to them, leaving the other side to look for theirs. If they get a ' counsel's opinion' to protect them-selves, don't mind it. Anybody can get that by stating the facts his own way. And a 'counsel's opinion ' isn't a judgment It isn't even evidence. It only means what he would say if he were a judge, given the amount of information vouchsafed to him. Another judge might say the opposite, and then three more might come and contradict them both ; and very often do. Remember, too, if you have the opportu-nity, to make your case as you intend it to be—being, as it is, yours and not other peoples—by your own letters first Having the answers, fix your mind on the two or three, at the outside, to which nearly every case can really be reduced, and through your counsel stick to them. Let the other side confuse the issues by superfluous and misleading correspondence as they may, and if your judge be fair and capable, as it is his business to become, he will select those letters for the kernel of the case. But this presupposes that you have convinced yourself by logic, not by 'opinions,' that you are three times in the right If you doubt it, never go to law. There are other means by which you may get righted." Said, of course, in his staccato way, this was the summary of Westburian wisdom. I have tested it more than once, and in the end have seldom found it wrong. But the worst of it is, and appar ently always will be, that before you can get at the law you must get through the solicitors. Which shall not be if, with few fine exceptions, they can help it, for a mighty long time. For it is but solicitors' law, alas, that our law-abiding country mainly doth abide, And with a twinkle so Said Westbury.

And so from bar to stage again, from Kean to Kean, from father unto son, from Edmund unto Charles. Our families were close friends, of course, after that be-ginning, and he was. much at my father's table in my young boy-days, thereby, I think, dissipating for ever any fears of the woolsack that might have haunted my bar-doomed life. Annoyed with my mother, who was an invalid, unable to attend the theatres, because she admitted one evening that she had been to hear Albert Smith (his jealousies were always boyish), he carried me off to his theatre in re-venge, and introduced me to his Columbine, whose flounces and eyes settled my tastes definitively. He became so fond of me, and I of him, that I almost lived at the Princess's during the holidays. Early after breakfast I trotted off to rehearsal as if I were a child actor, and wandered at my will from box to stage, and stage to box Particularly when the ***Midsummer Night's Dream*** was being rehearsed, when all the pretty girls of the company, save when their scenes were on, collected in the Royal box and petted me. Kean had a wonderful eye for pretty girls Carlotta's crown of feature, and to think of her is to remember the critic's saying of Miss Foote's Virginia, that attract and Romanise you as she might, there was always "a delightful touch of the English school-girl in her acting." Kate Terry's acting was all light, expression, and intelligence, the movements free and graceful as the " silvery-footed antelope's," and the voice appealed to you at once through the tears that lay hidden in its tones. Such a Prince Arthur, such an Ariel such a Titania when at the end she took La Carlotta's part. If less of beauty, more of grace and mind. Her

Cordelia, played when she was still but a child in years—as indeed to the end of the Kean management she was—even then was quite a memorable thing, and the first I remember of her as a personality was when Kean told us in the green-room that he could make the child cry as he liked by reading her the scenes of Lear. Of all the actresses of my English day, to the end Kate Terry, with Helen Faucit her fore-runner, will remain my favourite and first choice. Both reached their greatest fame at twenty-three. The acquaintance thus begun in behind-the-scenes boy-and-childhood grew into a very close and loving friendship with her family, and led to my playing many parts as an amateur with her and the still younger Nelly, who by right of her adorable impulse was to grow into the first stage-favourite of the town, in the years then hidden in the folds. Her first I saw as " Puck "—a child—rising through the stage upon a toadstool, like incarnate mischief. And I think that the feat has lent a kind of Pixie-flavour, ever since, to all the scenes of comedy that she has played. Both Kate and she commingled tears and laughter charmingly. But Nelly's gift was laughter. Kate's was tears. In-finitely funny were many of the stage-adventures that we all had together. Too many for a record that must cover so much ground. But one was memorable. We played for some distress about something that was going on in Lancashire. I think that it had to do with cotton and the American war. Anyhow it was one of those charitable calls for self-sacrifice which the amateur actor always feels so acutely. Our theatre was a big theatre. For, to rise to a great occasion, our committee took Covent Garden. And our play was a small play, meant for a small stage It was The Lighthouse, a thrilling little melodrama by Wilkie Collins. And Palgrave Simpson and I enacted the two Gurnocks, father and son. And the curtain rose on the first act, and discovered us with our two heads in our four hands, on the two opposite ends of a sea-chest, cut off from " land " in a lighthouse, and starving by our two selves. My part was the inevitable "young first," for which, in days of romantic slimness, I was always cast Therefore it was a very bad one. But through an awk-ward failure on the author's part, I never left the stage for a minute through the whole play. We had not had a single rehearsal in the big house, to accustom us to the size, and when the curtain rose, the public, who had not seen our charitable intentions in a proper light, filled, at a liberal guess, about one-tenth of it. I gazed upon the sparsely populated district as I raised my head, and spake. If I had not in those days learned to modulate my voice, I was possessed at all events of what is called an organ. To be heard on the stage is everything. And I wish that a few more players thought so nowadays. So I projected my young chest, inflated my young lungs, and, fixing with my eye the farthest-off straggler whom I could dimly discern in the gloom (after a piece of advice once given me by Alfred Wigan) I intoned as through a fancy speaking-trumpet: " I've had no food for many days, and I'm so weak that I can scarcely speak." My spirit must have prevailed over my flesh: for my little all all heard me.

Later on came my climax, in that strange ordeal of discomfort. I had to open a bay-window, and the sea was to dash in. It was to be soap-suds by a new invention, with a great deal of wind. Through the bay the ocean was expected to enter. I went towards that window. The bay was still there, but the soap-suds were gone. " Look out for the dash of the spray, Martin," said my father Aaron. So I did ; but it wasn't there. " Much wind but no soap-suds," thought I. I must pretend. So I retired into the bay out of sight of the audience, to come back pretending. But as I did so an ancient woman rose behind that window, with a huge wooden bowl in her hands, having entirely missed her cue. And without a moment's warning she hurled the whole contents into my face. The audience didn't see it Nor did I. Blind, spluttering, choking, staggering, I got back into my seat just as my sweetheart Kate Terry arrived in a boat to save me. She rushed upon her Martin to enfold him in a stage embrace. All I could do was to croak out in the hoarsest tones, under what breath that dash of the spray had left me, " For the Lord's sake don't kiss me I I am only soap."

CHAPTER VIII

ABOUT THE ACTING OF CHARLES KEAN AND FECHTER

CHARLES KEAN was not the first man who has suffered from being a great man's son. Nor will he be the last. He was not Edmund to Edmund's worshippers, whose name was legion. Therefore, he was a fraud. But he suffered from another cause : the unfair and ruthless onslaughts of the Press, goaded and led in *Punch's* pages by Douglas Jerrold. Charles Kean was all that was great and good, until he produced a very bad play of Jerrold's called *St. Cupid, or Dorothy's Fortune,* but declined to act in .it himself. He kept faith by producing it, but that was not good enough. And from that hour forward Jerrold hounded him down, and the Press, too easily led then in that way, did nothing but always sneer at him. Jerrold's was a biting but merely ill-natured wit, of which all the best sayings recorded are only rude and cruel It is a cheap and easy form of it, at best One specimen will serve. Thackeray was one of his own colleagues upon *Punch,* a head and shoulders taller than him and everybody else, which he did not appreciate. And when at a large gathering, Thackeray said that he was going to make a present to a small god-child, after his own unfailing views of humour, Jerrold's polite remark was: " Don't give him your own ` mug.'" Funny, but about as true as it was kind. And it may serve as a standard for all the little gentleman's wit Subject to the same physical and moral inferiority as the great but spiteful poet of Twickenham, Jerrold was a Brummagem Pope, without the genius or the fancy. But his unkind tongue has done Charles Kean's fame a mischief ever since, as Pope's did Cibber. Yet neither Cibber nor Kean was a small man at all. And, with whatever in me lies, out of love for the ac-tor's art, I, who remember the latter's work so well, am glad to write of it while there is yet the time.

As a matter of fact, Charles Kean remains to me one of the most magnetic ac-tors of my day. Magnetism can repel as well as attract, so about him as about Irving, who has been gifted before all things with the same master-quality, difference of opinion flourished very widely. With a short though well-knit figure and a plain face, none the less all his movements were free and elegant as became a captain of the Eton boats, and the face could assume expressions that made it charm-ing. The smile was exquisite. The voice was harsh but clear, and easily charged with pathos or with humour. His fencing was a sight to watch; and in earlier days than I can remember, so good a judge as Sala could speak of his Prince of Denmark as the most tenderly romantic he had seen. He could even lend quite a singular charm to such a part as Evelyn in *Money,* and such a Shylock certainly I never saw. The grim humour, concentrated force, and inexorable purpose of the man never found a truer outlet Nor did Kean make the mistake of trying to secure an impossible sympathy for so mere a monster, a man who comes into court deliberately to cut away a pound of flesh from another's heart, because he wouldn't ask interest on his loans. Furious for the wrongs of his race, no doubt, but not of his religion, which he talked so much about He was ready to change it at the last moment and all at once, to save half his money. Yet the sympathy which so many want to claim for such a creature is always reduced to one passage, from which he appears to have once given his wife a turquoise, which his daughter stole, and to have missed it considerably.

Mrs. Charles Kean, whom as Ellen Tree, of course, I do not remember, was the more famous artist of the two when the two were married. But like the good woman and good wife that before all she was, she was from that hour content to sink herself for him, and to shine but with a reflected glory, the greater for the absolute and touching confidence with which he repaid her. How funny he was with her at rehearsals. " Seek Mrs. Kcad!" if anything went wrong. "Oh Elled, Elled! take that man out of the front rank, and put him at the back! His legs must not be seen. No, no, my good man, it's not your fault, but we can't help these things." "Oh Elled, Elled! I wanted a full-dress rehearsal. And the Archbishop of Canterbury has come without his bitre." She acted up to Kean so finely, always in the picture, quiet but in harmony. Her Portia and his Shylock made each other. She was too old for the part when I saw them, but it didn't matter. Mrs. Kean's Portia took no interest in Antonio whatsoever. She knew that he was safe. Her interest was in Shylock. "Is your name Shylock ? " as she looked him up and down, to see if there could be within the compass of humanity any man set upon so cold-blooded a murder as that. She would do all that in a woman lay, to save so dark a soul. Her `` quality of mercy " was no set speech. It was a lawyer s plea, beautifully woven with all the high appeals. She pleaded with Shy-lock through his feelings ; through his interest ; through his avarice ; through everything, with a patience all untired. In vain. Then she turned round in wrath, a woman and a goddess, standing like a classic statue at the tribunal's foot " Tarry a little! there is something else!" And from that moment, not another pause—in that indignant soul. " He shall have merely justice—and his bond." Yet at the last, by one supreme womanly touch of the incomparable Master, she melts again, and appeals to the merchant's feeling as her guide. She has none left but one, at all. "What mercy *can you* render him, Antonio?" And what the generous Merchant of Venice offers—the gentle, gentlemanlike, central figure, whose value the theatre never understands—so Portia does. Here endeth the greatest play seen in the world. All manhood and all womanhood in that one little compass. All passions and all feelings—all love, friendship, hatred, pity, spite, vengeance, apostasy, and murder: brain, law, argument, patience, irritation, religion, humour, scorn.

I must have paid Charles Kean out for that introduction to his Columbine. How good to her he was, as he was to everybody round him. She fell into an illness of weakness soon after she had been promoted to the part, and he lost her services. But finding that a family was dependent on her, he not only paid her full salary all the time, but provided her with the best stout, which her doctor ordered her to drink, and sent her to the sea when well enough. But for me, I became the terrible infant or chartered libertine of the theatre. On my way to the last train for Harrow or for Oxford, I would jump out of my cab, and in my tall hat and a mask " go on" with the crowd in the masked-ball scene of the *Corsican Brothers,* or hide behind the skirts of the girls in the Royal box under suppressed laughter when *Henry the Fifth* was being rehearsed, and Kean would call out, " I know it's that boy. Take him away. He's upsetting my whole arby." Or appear behind the scenes at a wrong moment during the performance, and be rushed at by the great manager with, " Go away, I'll tell your father!" Which he never did. He was a lovable friend and man ; and I often went after breakfast to his house in Hyde Park Street, when the theatre spared me the self-imposed duties of re-hearsals which would have done without me, for the delight of a good talk with Mrs. Kean and him. One morning I found him fuming up and down. " What's the matter, Mr. Kean?" "The matter! Have you seen the papers?" "Yes, why?" "There's a new fellow come out in Hamlet" " Oh yes,

Dillon." " Dillod ! that's his — name. Confound him ! " " But why shouldn't he ? " " Why shouldn't he ? Why, in my father's time, if anybody had attempted to act one of his great parts in London, all the papers would have been down upon the man for his impudence. None of them has mentioned me this morning! " " Pardon me, Mr. Kean, I did see one." " Did you ? what did it say?" I saw oil on the waters. " It said," I told him, " that it was rash for any man to play Hamlet in London when

there were two such tragedians on the stage as Kean and —" "And Phelps, I suppose! He can't play the part a damn !" So, like that of the foolish virgins, my oil went
out.

He loved to show me the workings of his ship, as he called his cherished Princess's, and all the mechanical arts and devices by which, by the ingenuity of Oscar
Byrne, he succeeded in putting so confined a stage to such elastic use. To make up for
its shallowness, he first invented the notion of the scene set slantwise, to give depth
through perspective; and, when one thinks of the vast strides made since by the arts
of lighting and decoration, the use to which he turned his limited materials is wonderful to look back upon. Neither by the Saxe - Meiningen company nor any other,
I think, has his stage-management of crowds been ever bettered. And as Charles
Kean was a great and accomplished antiquarian, he was able to carry out his own
designs without the advice of sculptor or of artist, especially in the great historical
" revivals "—as it became the odd fashion to talk of plays which, never dying, can
never be revived—in which he made a great advance upon Macready, and no man
since has ever been able to advance on him. He made his Ariels and angels float in
the apparent air by a mechanical contrivance all his own. Kneeling on a solid perch
hidden by gauze at the back, which glided up and down a groove, and was covered
by long trains or petticoats, they were a puzzle always to the audience; and the
apotheosis of Marguerite in *Faust,* as a vision of Carlotta Leclercq's peerless beauty,
was of all stage pictures one of the most memorable. It was a little dis-enchanting to
such a young outsider, perhaps, to see these mysteries at work from behind, and on
one occasion, when six angels ap-peared to Queen Katharine in a vision in *Henry
VIII.*, I was the witness of a sad catastrophe. There were six of them sliding on in-
visible perches up and down a sunbeam. They were all pretty, and nicely graduated
in years and height, so that the topmost angel was a little child. With keen youthful
interest I watched them being tied on their perches in a kneeling attitude, and then
draped with gauzy flowing mysteries till they all seemed sitting upon nothing. Then
the soft music began to play, and the pulleys to work them up and down, and the
gauzes to be withdrawn which were between them and Queen Katharine's dying
couch; and then they began to sway their bodies and to wave their arms ; and then
the little child-angel at top, who had been eating too many oranges, began to feel

the motion and was rather sick; and the girl-and-women angels down below her, descending as it were from heaven in a bee-line, disliked it very much ; and they ministered to the poor Queen that night in but a half-hearted sort of way, particularly when the audience encored the vision.

After a celestial experience such as that, it was but earthy to be taken by Kean to the regions overhead one morning, to see his new thunderstorm, then raging every night. Over a floor above the stage was spread a sheet of iron, and in the corner, revolving on a pivot, a mighty box all full of cannon-balls. You had but to tip the box and the storm came on. It burst in a sudden crash with all the cannon-balls, then growled itself out in declining fury as they ran about the floor. " You must be very quiet, my boy," said Kean, " as they are rehearsing the new farce underneath." Whereupon with true Harrovian instinct I said, "Yes," and tipped the box immediately. I have been in the middle of severe thunderstorms amongst the Alps and elsewhere, but never in one like that I made myself. The thunder had all to be collected again, and as no lightning had introduced it in the usual polite way to the company downstairs they nearly all had fits. The stage-manager and prompter leaped headlong up to the flies by the first stairs they could get at, scenting some awful catastrophe to the machinery. And dear old Charles Kean, most childishly amused of mortals when anything upset his gravity, sat down amongst the cannon-balls and laughed till he couldn'tSee.

His ***Corsican Brothers*** and ***Louis the Eleventh*** were, I think, the crown of his achievements as an actor. Nobody ever touched him in the first So stern and picturesque an embodiment of a remorseless fate as he, when he came face to face with his brother's slayer in the last act, never crossed the stage. So intensely calm and so unutterably still, intensity in its true sense was Charles Kean's force. When he had broken his sword in two to match his enemy's, and wound his handkerchief round the steel point and his wrist, he never took his eye off Château-Renaud's face, or moved one muscle of his own. Nor did he stir one inch from

the place where he had taken stand. He simply turned and turned again upon his heel to face the duellist, who was round him, about him, savage and anxious and alert, everywhere—striking at Fabien fiercely, over and over again, to have the stroke turned easily aside, and always, by that iron wrist, Kean struck once, and once only, as the fate-clock of the forest rang the hour. And in a mass, and in a moment, Chateau-Renaud fell at his feet stone dead, like the chieftains in Macaulay's lay. Usually unequal, seldom playing anything so well that there was not * something weak in it, seldom anything so ill that it had nothing great, Charles Kean was on the whole, I think, at once the greatest master of the drier humours, and in his best parts the most impressive actor I ever saw. And he knew the force of contrast. Himself a small though splendidly knit man, he liked a big Château-Renaud, who towered well above him, and looked as if he could break him in his hand. Fechter was a mere fidget in that double-character, after him.

Louis XL. was a greater feat; the actor's greatest; for he made himself the man. I am by no means sure that it isn't one of living's greatest achievements, too, showing how differently two great actors may read the same part For except the grim humour shown in different ways, the two bear no resemblance. Irving might almost have studied the avoidance of Kean's points, and the invention of his own, from Kean, but that he never saw him in the part. Irving is the more subtle. Kean was the more intense. There never was a false note or feature in that picture all the way. Familiar, cruel, superstitious, weak yet strong, fearful and obstinate, a king through all. He made to himself a wonderful walk for the part which was all his own, a kind of trot which was almost a run, yet curiously natural. He had studied the character from the book of "Quentin Durward," and his portrait had nothing in common with the work of the French actors, Ligier or Beauvallet, both far his inferiors in the part He thought .Qut every detail to a fascinating whole, incarnate cruelty being his starting-point, and the result remains alive with me to this hour, full-grown Velasquez. I used to go and see it so often that the great man grew suspicious of Carlotta Leclercq's attractions, as the Dauphin, for my youthful mind. Certainly never did maid wear the lovely garnish of a boy more beautifully. " Herbad," he said, " you're rather precocious, you dow. I don't believe you come here to see be at all. It's Biss Leclercq's legs." To a certain extent, I'm not sure that it wasn't true. They had their charm.

Every really great actor leaves a name, chiefly associated with one part, and not a part from Shakespeare. We all discuss their Hamlets and their Richards, but Kemble's ***Cato,*** Macready's ***Richelieu***, Phelps' ***Sir Pertinax,*** Kean's ***Louis XL***, Booth's ***Foots Revenge***, Irving's ***Bells?*** Is not the reason pretty clear? Shakespeare is too great. It is literal fact that his greatness has distinctly injured, and not helped, the progress of the playwright's art in England. It sets up in the poetry of it an Elizabethan standard to begin with, which cannot be pulled down by the boldest Victorian raider. All men who aim at the highest in the art are brought to the one comparison. It is like standing up for electrocution. And managers that speechify maunder all over the place about the "coming man/' for whom they wait, helping thereby the poor old cant about the lack of dramatists, which never changes, and riseth from the hearts and pens of the great multitude of ready writers, who want to indite plays and cannot Their own are all right, of course, each speaking for him or herself, the next and greatest need being to get somebody else to think so. The maun-derers mean that they want another Shakespeare. Well, they won't get him. There will be a new drama when there is another Shakespeare. There will be a new religion when there is another Bible. Be thankful for what you have, and don't be always sneering. Sneering is, in itself, proof positive of conscious inferiority.

As with the authors, so with the actors. Shakespeare crushes. The best of them struggle under such a weight of language, like Tarpeia under the golden ornaments. The very words exhaust all human passion. What is there to add ? But it is the actor's work to add, not by the unwholesome thing called gagging—though even that is sometimes not without its use—but by interpreta-tion and by thought. There is a story of a French author who grew very uncomfortable when Bouflé was rehearsing a character of his. The actor asked him if he had any fault to find. "Mais, Monsieur, vous n'ajoutez rien!" he said. With Shakespeare, ***on n'ajoute pas.***

Singular that to this rule I recall one exception, and that, to his honour be it said, a Frenchman. Fechter's appearance as an English actor followed shortly after Charles Kean's retirement from management, and, too soon, from life. And Kean was more amusing about " that Frenchman " than about anything else. His own French, it must be admitted, was purest Captain of the Boats. " Shattow-Reddow," with a strong emphasis on the first syllables, was his way of dwelling on the duellist, whom Fechter dismissed as " Châteaurenaud " all in one syllable, as the man of Killarney contrived to do, they say, with McGillicuddy's Reeks. That any Frenchman should act in English at all was too much for that Etonian spirit But that he should act any of his—Kean's—parts, was sacrilege. Why, it was worse than " Dillod" Some rash intruder accused Kean of having had hints from Fechter about his Mephistopheles — a strong stage picture of the popular fiend from the jocular stand-point, but memorable—and he admitted it with a reservation. When he grew excited, his m's and n's were wont to get more mixed than ever with him. " Taught me, did he ? Dab his impudence. I went to see him in Paris, and he showed me how to bake by dose."

Nevertheless, it is by right of his Hamlet and Iago that Fechter takes his rank with me. Of all my actors of romance he was the best, and in that light he made those parts quite daringly his own. It has been told of " W. G." the cricketer, that when he made his first appearance at Brighton with his new methods, Alfred Shaw the bowler, after the match was over, complained to an old chum— the umpire, who had not seen Grace before— that he never bowled so well in his life, and that he was always being hit for four or six against the rules. "It's all very well," he said, "but it ain't cricket" "Well, Alfred, I dunno," answered the pal. " If you bowls

him all you knows, and he cobs you out of the ground every time, I calls it cricket, and —— good cricket too/' So did an astonished world remark of Fechter's Hamlet that it was very wonderful, but wasn't Shakespeare. Well, perhaps not, though only Shakespeare knows. But if a Hamlet fairly sweeps you off your feet in a whirl of new excitement, in the scenes in which you have been most accustomed to methods of quite another kind, I call it Shakespeare, and   good Shakespeare too. My umpire in this case was a quaint old box-keeper who had served under Kean, and remained at the Princess's when Fechter was there. Of course we were old friends, and when I went to see the Frenchman's Hamlet, I asked him what he thought about it before the play began. " Sir!" he said, "it's wonderful. We all know Mr. Kean. Mr. Kean was great. But with 'im, `*AmUt* was a tragedy, with Mr. Fechter it's quite another thing. He has raised it to a meller-dram." And in its stirring sense of action, with his vivid stage-management, and with his romantic, volcanic, lawless personality, that is exactly what Mr. Fechter did.

His Iago was another thing, and about that there could be no mistake. It was Shakespeare, and for the first time; the everybody's friend, the honest Iago of the poet's words. I have his photograph in the part upon the wall behind me, and it should stand for a picture of Iago, with no name attached. There never was such a portraiture of the sheer triumph of mocking intellectual power. Of all Shakespeare's tragedies ***Othello*** is the weakest, for all its glorious wealth of poetry and tongue. The motive is so weak. So all unlike the motive power of ***Lear or Romeo, Hamlet or Macbeth***. " And all that for a pocket-handkerchief!" (E tutto questo per un fazzoletto!) was the Italian lady's comment when she saw the play.' A question not only of the harmless necessary cicerone, but such a widely Platonic one! Everything happens without excuse. Othello is an ass—Desdemona an idiot—Iago a knave. Iago's knavery, therefore, must rise out of sheer exuberance of almost physical delight, and a very athleticism of unscrupulous roguery. He makes his fools his purses, and his dumb-bells too, and all of them. His is the central figure rightly played, as Boito discovered whenhe wrote his poem forVerdu And without obtruding himself for a minute on the scene unduly, Fechter played it so. They were his puppets, all the rest, until Emilia turns, in the one scene which, because it is so superbly human, is the most powerful in all the play, and gives the lucky actress of that little part the much-loved "sympathy" denied to all the rest. Even so has many a Macduff, to the disgust of many a Macbeth, found himself the astonished hero of the hour. From the moment of Emilia's burst, which found him out, Iago held his tongue. And Fechter held it with a face, not of baffled villainy, but of conquering contempt Once, after the council scene, he stayed alone upon the stage, behind the rest, and having it all to himself broke into one clear laugh of triumphant enjoyment. Then sharply turned, and put his finger to his lips, and went His gestures in the part were extraordinary, simply. His pantomime alone, lightning-like, would have made clear the meaning of the speech.

That I should wear my heart upon my sleeve For daws to peck at.

English actors are seriously hampered, as against the much-puffed foreign im-porta-tions, by the fact that Englishmen do not gesticulate, and that of acting gesticulation is the life. For us, the less of it the better. But Fechter, born of an Alsatian father, had an English mother, and came from Hanway Yard. Though his accent was marked, his speech was clear, and his English scholar-ship perfect He knew his Shakespeare through. And with him, appropriate gesture was a part of his personality.

When Charles Kean retired from manage-ment, and went for an acting-tour round the world, a serious undertaking then, he wanted me to go as one of the two actors whom he took with him, as his Horatio or Laertes, Bassanio or Gratiano, or what not I wavered, balanced, wished: but I was young and the transition strong, and I let it go for what it might have been worth. I wonder, was I wrong? I like to remember the Keans most, I think, when they came out from Exeter where they were acting, to dine one Sunday evening at my grandmother's, a country house some two miles distant An hour or so before they came, a country parson-cousin of the true Devonian type came out to call. He was very eccentric, told wonderful stories, and would have made his fortune as an actor. His son, heredity-condemned, went on the stage in after years, James Nutcombe Gould, and made himself a good name of his own before he was too soon lost to us. But he would not have touched his father. When my grandmother began to fidget as Parson Gould stayed on, he asked if anybody was coming to dinner. She said the Keans. So he said he would stay. My grandmother, convinced that he was dangerous—for she was very nervous— consulted me as to what she should say to the Keans. I suggested that she should say nothing, and that they would get on capitally. But conscience induced her to take Mrs. Kean aside, and warn her that the other guest was most eccentric. Kean, being warned, too, grew nervous, and dramatically fixed the parson with his eye. But one anecdote told another, and one joke certified another; his new acquaintance became too much for him altogether, and they were as merely boys as I was. It ended in Manager Kean offering Parson Gould anything he liked, if he would but accept an engagement Parson Gould would have been right glad to do it Dear old Devonshire home, now gone away from me with all the rest I have had good times with you in many ways, in spite of Fate. It was long after that that when she was very old, my grandmother suddenly asked me how old I was. I told her. " Oh! But then it's quite time for you to marry." " So it is, grandmamma Have you anybody to suggest?" "I don't know. But I could find out. Oh, but I forgot You've taken to play-acting or something like it, haven't you. Of course you can't expect to marry among the gentry now." Dear old-world ladies of Jane Austen's school. For how long yet will you be with us ?

CHAPTER IX

ABOUT MY BOYHOOD AND LITTLE DOTHEBOYS

YES, it was a quaint change of life at that age, to turn suddenly from a Corsican Brother masquer at the Princess's to a good little boy at Harrow. For I believe I was a good boy, when I was left to myself; at all events harmless. I never got flogged, or did anything dreadful. But I was very lonely, and felt a good deal of sympathy when I read of Anthony Trollope's sufferings and experience at the same school The mistake in my case was entirely of home commission, and was a hard one. I was forced, and a year too young for my place, all through. Even my Balliol matriculation came six months too soon. And a spirit for ever struggling, first against the classical and then the legal, bars—while always pining

for free literary emancipation, has but a fourth dimension kind of a time of it I could even draw inspiration on the subject from the New Mystics of the day, and relapse into the Freemasonry of Pythagoras, whose followers knew each other by strange turns of thumb, and looked for guidance and inspiration to the Worshipful Master of their Lodge, whose creed of Creation was Harmony—whose keys to it, Music and Numbers, whose cosmos filled the space between the moon and the fixed stars—whose Heaven lay between the moon and earth, whose source of life was fire, with the central fire for Universe's Hub. I might imagine myself to have lived before in the congenial days of Horace, and have walked down Sacred Street according to my custom, meditating trifles I know not what, and all in them, but, unlike him, needy, and out of work, and stopping at the columns, or book-seller's shop, to pick up a second-hand papyrus cheap, or ask if anybody wanted a translation from the Greek on modest terms. If, however, I have ever had glimpses of a previous existence myself, they have been usually after dinner, and the matter-of-fact element in my composition militates terribly against the new brotherhoods. In fact, I cannot but agnize a certain mental flabbiness in this the twentieth Age of Messianic Era, mainly to be detected in an unwholesome crop of double surnames betokening a kind of hesitating and general uncertainty of men as to what they really think, impartially sown along the various paths of life. Chris-tian-Scientists, Anglo-Catholics, Liberal-Imperialists, Liberal - Unionists, Conserva-tive-Democrats, Garden-Architects, all seem rather representative of the Age of the Mixed Ideas.

Oh, sympathetic reader, should I meet with one, you will feel that mine was not a happy boyhood, in spite of Thespian excitements none too wise at that age. All very well perhaps, if instead of turning actor or even scribe, the authorities had not insisted on my making a lawyer of myself. Love-lessness and violent bickerings on the hearth are not a healthy school, and I was a good deal worn out with it before my days of adolescence. I do not on reflection recognise mine either as an unkindly or ungenerous nature, but "Put him out of the way anywhere" was always the family device where my poor person was concerned. So it is now, for the unnatural tradition has been thoroughly well kept And up to sixteen or thereabouts I was a very small person indeed. Precocity appears to have been my sin, and it is a fearful nuisance. But it was not my fault if I was set on tables to recite—usually " Young Lochinvar," or selections from the " Battle of the Lake Regillus." I recite the last in private still in hours of weakness. But I must have been a rather dreadful boy, through no fault of my own, at moments such as these. Only the other day I met again a very old lady, who remembers me well in those days, and heard me. And she says I was. Nor was precocity sufficient reason for robbing an imaginative child of all home influence, for what it might have been worth, and of all home care when he was only eight years old, and pitching him headforemost into a private school of the Dotheboys order, commoner in those days than I hope they may be now. I was far the youngest and smallest of all the young and small boys there, and to this hour I can recall my heart-breaking sobs at evening, when I found myself in the garden of the school-house all alone, the servant who had brought the new boy down having departed for the home that had cast forth his infancy. It was weak of me to cry; unmanly, the schoolmistress that very night informed me with a glare through spectacles. But I was only eight

The discipline of that uncomfortable place did not improve my early battered nerve, shaken at its most sensitive period by such cold, hard measure from the authorities at home. The master and mistress of the delectable academy might upon such precedent be excused, perhaps, if they regarded me as a plant worth neither cherishing nor tending. But their joint effect was singularly bad on everybody. One of my fellow sufferers there, a fine fellow and an able one, who died in the after years with a disordered mind, said steadily and always that his temper never recovered the effects of that private school. Nor has mine, ever, for temper turns on nerve. And nerve on training, subject to constitution, which in my case happily both stood and stands, through everything that nearest and dearest with the help of a bosom friend could or can do to kill it, illogically strong and cheery as it was. But then, in my case, as compensation rules in all things, marriage was to prove, after long years of one unbroken trial, the reward for all and more. And oh, how the nearest and dearest cried out upon that marriage, and would have stopped it if they could But as it so happened that at that crisis of my life my n's and d's—but female then, my father being dead—had lovingly deserted me in illness they had caused, and left me to sink or swim with a fervent aspiration for the first, they were not in a position to forbid the banns. My ladye was not afraid, and took me up. But my family affections take some colour from Thackeray and The Newcomes.

Of course I was bullied at Little Dothe-boys, badly and righteously. I don't complain of that, it's boy-humanity. And I suppose that boy-nature in those respects is best set forth in the little fellow who was taken to the bosom of the kind old lady who condoled with him when he poured forth his complaints about being `` tunded" by the big boys at school. " Never mind, dear, the lesson will do you good. When you're a big boy in your turn you won't tund the little ones." "Oh won't I?" I was well tunded, certainly, and the schoolmistress began it My poor little games of imagination were all stopped. " Thank goodness," said a relative who shall be nameless, of my weaknesses in that way, "we knocked all that nonsense out of him." And indeed they did, for a time and for a long time. But the result of expelling Nature with a fork was long ago proverbial. It would crop up again. Even if my bricks were impermissible—it seems so odd to me to think that I was only eight, when I was turned out of home to be so ruthlessly suppressed in this way—I should have liked my toy-stage, with paper figures, on which I tried to produce my miniature tragedy. Finding it ineffective as an acting play, I fell back upon **Grindoff; or the Miller and his Men.** Such mischievous pastimes were no more for me, and I ground the classical mill of those days with a very weak and early hand indeed, and even with a weaker and a lesser heart I wonder often how I ever learned to love and to write plain English in spite of destiny. But it was always my one ambition, and somehow I think I do.

The schoolmaster of Little Dotheboys, of whom let me speak respectfully as Wanks, as a name that can injure nobody, was a weak and gentle, handsome and generally ignorant clergyman. His wife, my schoolmistress, and so to speak our boss, was his elder; coarse, strong, and loud, and usually a little drunk-Ushers supplied the learning as best they could. There were no young male Wankses, but four young female, all in residence. The boss began on me at once by cuffing me hard on the head at a very early stage of my school career, for hooking my paint-box on a Sunday. And when I murmured "Oh dear!" under my youthful breath, she vowed I said " Oh damn ! "—I don't think I then knew the expression—and ever after I was viewed as an early and hardened reprobate. I was so much talked about from this point of view before I was nine, that I began to believe in my own wickedness. Everything in my story so far would go to prove that I was, and am, a very bad character indeed; and unless others are, I must be. At that stage I had little left to do but glory in my evil, and, Iago-like, I assumed a scowl. It grew into a dangerous habit I have never quite lost, and made me in early youth solitary and unpopular. I didn't make a friend in the world, I think, before my Oxford days, with the strange exception of my beloved Harrow head-master, Dr. Vaughan, unless it was Charles Kean, and the two nurslings of his who are so still. No wonder either, for I was young and sensitive, and too entirely cowed. How I did loathe that preparatory school—preparatory, thank heaven, for a life that was not to be. Mine has not been, and was not, a dull one, or an unhappy one, after all. Was it not Pumas, the elder, who declared that the broad life of art and letters, with all its fights and drawbacks, was the one best worth living ? Throw in a dash of most things else all round, and in my case he was not far from right. There is enough of the vowel I in this, to begin with, but so it mote be. So there has been among most of the worthy gossips and egoists, to whom it is the purpose of this vivacious history to add another bore.

Shortly after that early castigation—Sunday if not Sabbatical for my soul's good, and so conducive to future Sunday observance for a child—in the absence of the much-crushed master the mistress studied my primitive Greek exercise. Even then I had learned something somehow. And she clouted my bothered little head more stunningly than before, for not having dotted my is and crossed my it's. I said that the Greeks didn't. She said I was a liar, for Greeks were not fools like me, and clouted me again. When Dominie came home he took my side with a submissive hesitation. He, too, said that the Greeks didn't She fiercely answered it was time they did. I must have been quite nine by that time.

I don't remember flogging at that school. The ceaseless torture was more deadly, more refined The food was good, and in appearance plentiful. Brimstone and treacle were not in the bond. But it was always removed when infant stomachs craved for it If such a poor little Oliver Twist as I suggested a thought more mutton, the lady thundered, " Take his plate away! He has had quite a pound of meat already!" The games of that Elysium I forget, except the "Rounders," which I vividly remember. Somebody threw a ball to me. If I hit it, fairly good. It was so thrown that if possible it might be missed, If I but missed it thrice, I had but to run as best I might, and for the nearest goal. Such as they were, my trousers were but tight below my little jacket, and an usher, standing behind the crease, hurled with much force a tennis-ball at the unprotected part, and rarely missed it. I didn't like that game. Oh children! children! what a time you had.

When we retired at eventide, Orientally we had to take off our shoes or boots, and place them on the. mat outside the door. Then we passed in reviewbefore the assembled family, and said, " Good-night, Mr. Wanks ; Good-night, Mrs. Wanks; Good-night, Miss Wanks; Good-night, Miss Jane Wanks; Good-night, Miss Amelia

Wanks; Good-night, Miss Thomasina Wanks ;" and got to bed. We were washed every Saturday night, that we might be clean for Sunday, and religiously disposed, in order to go twice to church, and pray from out our youthful hearts that all the nobility might be endued with grace, wisdom, and understanding. Like-wise the bishops, and the Houses of Parliament during their session. Out of the session, apparently, it didn't matter. To the fullest extent, our prayers have not so far been visibly answered. Anyhow, I do remember to this hour a certain rebellious feeling, that it couldn't matter much to me. I was wont to pray rather hard for my unlucky little self, but that was outside the business. The servant girls who washed our sinful bodies every Saturday were kind and sympathetic, as a rule, but scarcely in it. Upon their own accounts, they hadn't a good time.

Many years afterwards I visited as an old pupil that deadly place once more. Little Dotheboys was a desert, merely. Pupils there were few, if any. The school had gone to well-deserved grief. The grounds and parsonage looked small, and mean, and miserable, and deserted. I wondered from the heart of me how I could once have thought the space so large. Mr. and Mrs. Wanks were still there, but quite ineffably run to seed, and looking quarrelsome For Nemesis had fallen. They both made much of me, as I had then made something of a name, but I do not believe that either of them remembered me in the very least Apparently there were no hapless ushers left to keep the tradition of some learning up. Whither the various young ladies had departed I know not; to happiness I hope; for two of them at all events were not unkindly girls ; and Mr. and Mrs. Wanks both pleaded hard with me not to forget them, and to recommend the school, remembering what it had made of me ; and rather sore of heart I went away ; and from that hour have heard of them no more. In that uncomfortable nursery of mind and body I passed three wretched years.

Harrow? ah, why go on, except for Vaughan? Bullied and worried, more and more and more, in the fifth form when I was only twelve, I had to wear a tail-coat. My Exeter tailor made it, and said he never made one for so small a gentleman before. I walked with pride into the streets with it, and the Exeter boys jeered at me, very rightly. The Harrow boys at once pulled one tail off, and I went about in the other like a de-tailed cock. The doctor himself looked a little astonished, when after a keen examination he placed me in the upper stall, the highest to a new boy available; and when I went in to take my place there, "everybody larfed," as Thackeray says, and observed that there must be a mistake somewhere. Indeed, I think there was. It was May 1, 1851, and in the morning I had seen Paxton's exhibition opened; and after my instincts I was rather full of it All was a little sad and premature and hard, I think; and when many years afterwards I was cheered on the school steps, much to my astonishment, as an eminent Harrovian, side by side with a new-made bishop with whom I had driven down on Speech Day—"Bishop and dramatist, Iamb and lion together!" as Dr. Butler, head of the school when first I went there, said—it was like an odd, confused, and quite unlicensed dream. Most of my Harrow days, five years of them—I think I dreamed in my odd solitary soul away, except perhaps when we got up the principal scene of the Merchant of Venice, in Vaughan's house by permission, for boy performance, and Lord Spencer, a senior boy (Lord Althorp then), came in to gaze on me. " Which is the boy who knows Charles Kean?" he said. I was enacting Launcelot Gobbo, and thinking that I should have been cast for Shylock.

CHAPTER X

OF DR. VAUGHAN AND HARROW-ON-THE-HILL

WE played three scenes from the ***Merchant*** at that bold school show. The wager, the scene of the two Gobbos, and the trial. I think the Gobbos and 1 were imported, on the thrilling discovery that I knew Charles Kean at home. Otherwise I was of not much account But, once set up as an authority, I assumed much knowledge that I hadn't I was asked what an acting-manager was. I hadn't noticed that item on the play-bill at that age. So I affirmed at once that there were two—a tragic-acting-manager, and a comic-acting-manager. As Launcelot, I appointed myself the last, and Shylock by similar right assumed the other post I was asked what the Venetian council-room ought to be like. I replied that, as the case was one of life and death, the Doge's palace would have been all hung with black cash-mere as the proper thing, and cheap. Doges were always in Adriatic straits. Whereupon I had a line to myself in the programme, as having designed the scenes.

In my precocious daring I had done more than that. I wrote to the great Princess's manager to confide to him our plan, and asked him to tell me how we ought to dress. His kindly antiquarian spirit was moved to interest, and he wrote me many sheets of historical advice, which took my breath away. Some of us boys—a kind of inner cabinet— sat down in council over it, and agreed that on economical principles it was not to be done. Our Shy lock was a handsome boy, called Daniel, which moved our audience, when the night came, to the warmest applause of all. " A Daniel come to judgment, yea, a Daniel!" was the signal for uproarious applause, and it was generally voted that, as far as the bard was concerned, he had never written anything so good as that. Daniel-Shylock entirely declined the unbecoming garments suggested by Charles Kean, requiring something much more striking, to indicate, as he said, the character, and he finally appeared in an appropriate kind of conjurer's robe which his sisters made for him, all black, but profusely embroidered with little yellow devils and cross-bones, till he looked like a victim of the inquisition prepared for the Act of Faith. Which, of course, is exactly what the Jew ought to have been, and in his proper surroundings would have been. Our Portia was one of the irrepressible Ponsonbys, those gallant votaries of the stage and of the cricket-field; though my especial mate, in after days to become a dear friend now gone, was to find his line of work in a single-hearted and active devotion to the Church, A good man if there was one, but great company and a delightful humorist His youthful task was simple, as he appeared only in his lawyer guise. He borrowed of a rising junior the necessary wig and gown and bands, and addressed the Doge's Court in boyish mimicry as a man would the Recorder's, with one foot on a chair, his right fist pounding his brief as drawn up for him by Bellario who instructed him, his wig a little bit awry and his left hand underneath his gown behind him. "May it please yer, m'lud," was in every line of him, and in the mercy-speech one fairly missed a jury. The Venetian legal system was incomplete without it Our Dook was a great Dook, whose name in English flesh was Meade. He, too, followed forensic precedent by dressing as near a judge as he could, in a full-bottomed wig with a small gilt coronet on top and scarlet robes so heavy that he was uncomfortable in them when he moved. But he preserved his dignity by keeping as rigid on his seat, half-throne half-bench to point the double nature of the part, as he well could, and in one line, in spite of prompters, persisted in a reading of his own. He steadily refused to address the Jew according to the text, with:

Shylock, the world thinks, and I think so too.

With more respect for position than for rhythm he insisted upon substituting throughout :
Shylock, I think, and the world thinks so too.

As for myself the Launcelot, I took a cab from the paternal home in Westbourne Terrace and drove to a large ready-made clothier's establishment in the Edgware Road, where I invested in a huge rustic smock-frock coming down to the ankles and belted with leather at the waist The seller assured me that he supplied like garments in the gross to the village crowds at the Marylebone Theatre in Church Street hard by. And I think there was a play fitted; though, while figuring as Comic-Acting-Manager and Designer of Scenery on our playbill, I was perhaps not sorry to escape the responsi-bility of designer of costumes.

Our farce to follow was of course **Box and Cox**. Nobody ever presumed on anything else in those days. My dear old Fred. Ponsonby relieved his Portia by the printer Box, and a Hawkins, of much legal fame to follow, supplemented Gobbo Papa by Cox the Hatter. As Mrs. Bouncer I absolutely refused to figure, so Antonio did it. A good-looking and melancholy boy, to whom the merchant and the lady of the lodging-house came all as one. Melancholy being the key-note of both those human characters as drawn by master hands, that was as it should be. So—being as comic-acting-manager obliged to figure in the farce—I took the post of prompter, and sat in my smock-frock with the yellow book, under a convenient bracket with a tallow candle on it, which discoursed its troubles on me in bewildered streams till that hard hour was over. I was very glad when it was. But I honestly believe that I was among the first who were guilty of profaning a classic education with theatricals at Harrow, as I was at Balliol afterwards. Now they are part of the school curricle everywhere. For good or ill, who knoweth? Once encouraged in acting, school-boys care less for anything beside. Man's an acting animal, from cradle up. The evil masters do lives after them. They enjoy the acting.

I was lonely and not happy as a Harrow boy. The iron of that awful private school had entered too deeply into such a nervous child. 1 only got two prizes at Harrow, having but tried for three. In my English poem upon Westminster I ran a good second to George Trevelyan, who emancipated himself from the eight-syllable fetters when I dared not, and made a gallant dash into the ballad-metre of his uncle Macaulay. One of his couplets I remember now:

There the good Bishop of Bayeux unlike a bishop rode;
A milk-white steed of Flemish breed the iery priest bestrode.

Alas! what a loss it was to literature, when George Trevelyan took to politics. One of my own boy-couplets I remember too:

In one broad stream the fighting currents met,
And England crowned her first Plantagenet.

I carried off at Harrow the first of the modern-language prizes, finding myself in exactly the same perplexity as my bright ally, Max O'Rell, since then. When he was teaching at St Paul's, he was asked his terms for a series of lectures upon French and German. He answered—so much for French, though I forget what And for German ten times more. Applied to for his reason for so vast a difference he explained, " I should have to learn German." So had I. French from the first came natural to me, I don't know why. Not so the other tongue. And we had, at Harrow, to take up two languages. So I took off my coat for German with a month to do it in. Happily for me, our modern language master was a Briton, with very long red whiskers, and a gentle Briton too, who, as I have since then thought, knew very little about any languages at all. His was a mild nature, much played upon by naughty boys. Once when he was holding his class there was a talk of earthquakes in the papers. I fastened a string to one of the legs of his magisterial table, and gently jerked it as the lesson went on. He scratched his chin and gazed into the ceiling as was his wont, and said nothing. But he interviewed the headmaster, Dr. Vaughan, afterwards on the subject, on scientific grounds, assuring him that in full daylight he had experienced three slight but very distinct shocks of the earth, coming up through the legs of the table. The incident has ever since recalled to me the Pickwickian episode of Prodgers and the lantern. How that beloved headmaster chuckled when I told him. For, of course, I did. In French knew that I was safe when the modern language fight came on. But German—no. I managed to get through my examination upon paper passably enough, but when the dreaded ***vivd voce*** came? No matter, my earthquake friend was in the chair, divinely absent in his mind as always. He called on me to translate the passage from Schiller's " William Tell" about the storm. Whereat I stood up in my place, and in language of vigorous improvisation—for improvise I certainly could, in prose or in Verse either— declaimed all that I knew about the legend, the story of our first—and then only—William shooting the apple off his boy's head, in the market-place of Altorf. The other boys looked on in awe and ignorance, and I was too awake to give myself away. The master listened in a dream, and scratched his head. u Most excellent," he said. " I have not been able to detect the smallest trace of hesitation." And so I got full marks; and, afterwards, the prize. Conscience has gnawed at times till this confession.

My other prize was for reading aloud, when Trench, die archbishop's brother, gave one, A little hard on me, for at that hour my youthful voice was cracking, and at impassioned moments dashed into a squeak. And so discordantly, that after the first two essays of the whole sixth-form before Dr. Vaughan, I was placed on the retired list But the doctor was pre-eminently just, and on reflection gave me another chance. I took advantage of that chance, and won, by the most determined efforts after modulation. Murmur I might, but would not squeak again. Oh, but how quaint was that incomparable doctor over it. We read a chapter from Macaulay in succession. It fell to one boy's turn—a good little chap pre-eminent in cricket—to read the passage descriptive of Bentinck's devotion to his Dutch king William in illness. Pardon me for not remembering the exact words, but let us say they ran like this: " I could not want a glass of water, I could not want my pillow smoothed, but that Bentinck was always near me." With infinite and sarcastic disgust the boy declaimed it all the wrong way on, and in full tide of wrathful indignation. " I *could' t want a glass of water! I* couldn't *want my pillow smoothed, but* that *Bentinck was* always near me." The school-room shook with laughter, the doctor leading suit It was a curious contest that Boys were eliminated, one by one. Then Dr. Vaughan called in his counsellors, and it ended in three of us boys, for an hour and more by Harrow clock, reading aloud from Æschylus and Shakespeare and other of the deities, to three united Dominies sitting up in banc. Whence I alone survived; and, as for ever I shall gratefully remember, gratefully to the mightiest master of heart and language in the universal world, since somebody or something set it rolling, I owed it to my reading —cracked or no—of the shortest and most perfect love-scene upon earth, maybe in heaven either:

It was the nightingale, and not the lark!

Dear Dr. Vaughan! My master; more, my friend. It was a pain to him when I left Harrow just one year too soon, as just one year too soon I entered it. He hated my being taken away from him, for, as he often told me, he had not enough special time to devote to more than one or two, at the end, of those whom he believed to be his most promising scholars, and—I am not speaking without book—he believed that in another year he would have fashioned out of my lawless boyhood a classic scholar worthy of my forbears. Thanks to those forbears, only it was not to be; and honestly, with my unchartered love of English, I can't say I regret it But he made a friend of me. Night after night in my last Harrow summer, when the house was all abed, did he and I go out for night walks, round Harrow Park, and about Harrow Hill. In all the loving and delightful converse, which keen and listening youth like mine can hold with mature and humorous wisdom such as his. Oh—but he was humorous —to those who knew, he of the Rugby manner as we called it, bred in the school of Arnold, with the velvet glove hiding the iron hand. He, the one living instance of the "nolo episcopari," who refused Bishoprics one after another to hold upon his quiet way, yet in his steady pride of dignity, when he accepted for repose the post of Master of the Temple, for the first time taught the big wigs who

CHAPTER XI

HARROVIANA WITH DIGRESSIONS

I NEVER shall, and never could understand the principles on which I was educated. Why was I pitchforked into a had private school at eight? Why was I made a fifth-form Harrow boy, when I was only a nervous child of twelve ? Why was I withdrawn therefrom just when I was ripening under Vaughan, to matriculate at Balliol when I was not quite eighteen ? Why was I not discouraged more consistently—as I was not to be encouraged —in all sorts of literary and theatrical bargains, when at twenty-five I was to be, by an expensive modernism, dumped down at a Bar which from my heart and soul I loathed? Why was I permitted—nay, obliged—to live the extravagant life of an Oxford undergraduate of the day, with wines, and rides, and tennis-courts, and all die rest of it, and then mauled severely over the parental coals because I left college with a few—a very few— small debts behind me ? For ten years like a man I stuck to my detested calling, haunted always by an uneasy sense that I had no earthly business to be championing causes which I felt to be all wrong, with the same happy complacency as when I knew them to be all right. I wonder if that is why the lawyers never let their meetings pass without a general vindication of their virtues and a holding forth about their honour? Who's a-deniging of it, Betsy ? I stuck to it to please the home-authority which afterwards left me nothing at all in life to go on with, after so long a course of deliberately misdirected education. That money was spent on me like water there can be no doubt But it did me no good, being, as it were, mechanically done, as a presumed fulfilment of the whole duty of parents. Indeed, by the irony of fate, it seemed to take especial delight in being spent on the wrong thing. Expensive as need be was my whole legal curricle. First the chambers of a pleader and then those of a conveyancer, with agreeable attendances on the mysteries of the Courts of Law, and the wondrous series of Inns of Court dinners, by which the sucking barrister is, I suppose, held to eat wisdom into his mental parts, by road of stomach. And then the Western Circuit and Sessions, with expense more free than ever, the society of pleasant chums, claret and champagne for a favourite mess drink, and all things that make the budding lawyer's life so valuable a one. And when after a few years of casual briefing I came into a pleasant Httle junior's practice, it was in a specialty of Indian appeals in the Court of Privy Council, for the which all the pleading, and the conveyancing, and the dining, and the circuiting, and the humbugging, and the golden guineas lavished there-upon, had literally served no purpose whatsoever. And thus it was that, in spite of all this struggle against the grain, by follow-ing all the time in spite of me my own inveterate prepossessions, I feel myself to be, in spite of appearances and years of costly training in nothing, that person so much talked about, the man self-educate. I just taught myself, as best I could, what other's teaching left me time to learn.

I am not the only man of my time with whom the sink-or-swim business has been regarded as the shortest cut to education. I do remember one of a learned pundit who had two stalwart sons. " A very odd man, that," said one of his acquaintance. " He sends one of his boys into the navy to pre pare him for the Bar, and the other to Balliol to prepare him for the army." And I as I said made my first Harrow bow at twelve, to be made a butt of from the start. For I was in those days a mite even for my age, but placed by the doctor in the upper shell after a brief trot-out in Greek (Greek! at that hour of the day!) which was the highest place to which a new boy could aspire. I was agreeing with an early brother-Dotheboys, the other day, that somehow there must have been some seeds of learning sown at that early seminary, though as far as I can remember few of us picked them up; and when I was marched into the upper shell room—it was a week after the regular opening—the class-master regarded me through a magnifying-glass and marched me out again, saying that there must be some mistake. At the end of the first school term I was moved up into the fifth-form, which wears tail-coats of all absurd monstrosities.

Antony Trollope had no worse a time at Harrow, for I was very wretched. My first bedroom I shared with three scions of the nobility, as the novelists of that day called them. One young lord and two young honourables, and all three vied as to which could bully me the hardest, which has been perhaps the cause of subversive tendencies in the blood with me, ever since. In such strange ways does the world-stream mould characters. It was a little sad, all of it, I think, for I doubt if there is a harder lot in some ways in this world than being misunderstood, and I was always fretting. All the odder the contrast between that, and being presented about that time to Charles Kean's colubbide who patted me on the head and talked to me like Miss Fotheringay, in the wing by the prompter's box I doubt if that premature vision of pink silk tights at close quarters ever quite faded from my memory. Mostly I mooned away my time at Harrow, always in odd day-dreams about authorship, which were one day to come true within their limits; a more born scribbler never lived. When I have nothing else to write I have always written letters, and deeply mourn, in these degenerate days of typewriting, the disappearance of that pleasantest of figures, the correspondent-friend. Among women a few linger; amongst men, none. They nearly all write at you through their secretaries; and the secretaries, whose only business is to write, will but be rude through typewriters. I do detest playing literature on a sort of pianoforte. What delightful correspondences have I held, before those things came in, with such close friends as were to me George Bentley, the publisher, and Hutton of the old *Spectator.* The style of a typewriter, like his handwriting, is always just the same. Pens help a man to think, and English disappeareth with them. And so I mooned at Harrow, in the churchyard by Byron's tomb—and wondered at the epitaphs—particularly two, one on railway-guard called Port, who was run over on the line:

> Bright rose the dawn, and vigorous rose poor Port;
> Gay on the train he used his wonted sport.
> Before the eve his mangled form they bore,
> With pain distorted, and O'erwhelmed with gore.
> But when night came to close the fatal day,
> A ruthless corpse the gallant sufferer lay.

The other was reflective, but yet more wonderful.

> Remember me as you pass by;
> As you are now, so once was I.
> As I am now so you will be;

Remember Death and follow me.

Under which lines some most irreverent wag cut out an added couplet Thus :
To follow you I'm not content,
Unless I know which way you went

I wonder if those poems yet endure. But most I delighted in summer, to moon to and around Duck-Puddle, as our swimming-bath was called, where, as I always loved swimming, I used to bathe three or four times a day. Indeed I had forgotten amongst my school honours that I once won a prize for headers. " Ars ithyocephalica " or art of the straight head, the master who gave the prize christened it in choicest Græco-Latin, which even at that age offended my classical sense of propriety, very much. For if you take a header with a straight head, you break it, or at all events hurt it considerably. It's just what you mustn't do, except in Greek.

I loved my rackets, as afterwards my tennis, very dearly. My cricket a little, but not much. Football I loathed as horse-play, and because we were obliged to play it as part of the school course. Wherefore the little boys like me were treated by the big ones as so many extra footballs. I only liked the warm bath afterwards, and then the sausages and mashed potatoes at Parsons's stuffy little grub-shop down the hill by the cricket-ground; Parsons—long since gathered to his fathers and forgotten, having been a very odd old Harrow character indeed. He kept a kitten with six legs embalmed in a case, whereof he was most justly proud. Likewise he had a cunning knack at snuffing candles with his fingers, and swallowing the bits; and he had an aged wife who cooked the sausages before our eager eyes, and was as funny in her way as he was. He and one Billy Warner—a semi-cracked old boy who sold brandy-balls in a very long red coat with very large brass buttons—were the two town-patriarchs of my Harrow day.

Cricket—may I confess it ?—always a little bored me when I wasn't either batting or bowling. The fielding and crossing over when no balls came to you, seemed to my impatient soul something in the proportion of Falstaffs sack ; while the loafing about when your side was in and you wasn't, was even more difficult to get through. So my attain-ments didn't rise above my house-eleven. But I loved, as I do still, to watch a good game, and fell upon the very prime of Harrow cricket, when Billy Oxnham's hiouse could play the school, when Chandos Leigh and Kenelm Digby were the captains, and the mighty Walkers—precursors of the Graces and cricket-founders of the county of Middlesex, carried the cricket world before them. Great were the Billyites—thus called with base familiarity—in those days of the game; and great was the famous chaffing-gallery at Lord's, where once in every year, after the summer half or quarter, or whatever you called it, according to your schoolwas over, Eton and Harrow and Winchester met, in and out, for a whole week of battle.

It was in the early days of the Walkers that I joined the chaffers first upon that crazy gallery, outside the tennis-court, when that good old game meant beauty—the beauty of the bent body and the scythe-like stroke— and the ball killed dead by steely wrist and quiet skill, within the limit of the half-yard chase. Seven Walkers were they—in the land might none more mighty be—from J., the eldest, the big wicket-keeper, down to I. D. and the placid and elusive R. D., who, whether at rackets, or tennis, or cricket, always put the ball wherever you were not, and was wherever you put it I fought for rackets with him afterwards, at Oxford with all my wrist, and legs, and eye—I was rather pleased with myself when we began—and remember the state of heat in which I retired beaten right off, and the unperturbed coolness of the victor. So did another of these born game-players, an Austen Leigh, after completely exhausting a rival in two hours of Brighton tennis, with hair un-turned, and quite unconscious calm, remark, " Now I must go and take some exer-cise." The fourth of the brethren, A. H.f was one of the heroes of my first Harrow eleven, and remains on my mind as a boy who could do anything in the field, from bowling to keeping wicket at a pinch. I remember a long field throwing the ball up over his head, instead of to his hands, when he was doing so. Up shot the good right arm, and with the same sweep he caught the ball and cleared the bails off before the runner could get home. As for V. E., the flower of the whole flock, played for his fast round bowling, he broke down from overstrain at Harrow in the middle of an over, finished it by improvised lobs, and then and there became the lob-bowler of all time, till in a match between all England and the victorious Surrey of that day, I saw him go in late and make his hundred and eight runs—a big feat then—having begun by taking all the ten Surrey wickets with those deadly slows. When V. E. fielded at point orjjcover-point, I used to gaze and wonder what on earth he was made of. He was everywhere, and you might have said of him what was said of E. M. Grace, that there was nothing the man couldn't do except catch you at long stop—there were longstops in those days —off his own bowling. It didn't matter to V. E. at what part of his person the batsman hit the ball, or how hard he hit it. He caught it and kept it, and there an end.

It is an odd thing, a cricket memory. But curiously tenacious when you have watched the game. Playing in the Western Circuit team, I made acquaintance with an elder whose name attracted me some thirteen years after I had watched him from the chaffing-gallery. " You were the Winchester captain in the year blank," I said—I remember the year but shall not specify—" and you made sixty-five and forty-eight against Harrow, and one hundred and twenty-six and two against Eton." He admitted the impeachment, as even but three or four years ago I found myself at some chance hotel opposite a face I remembered, but for the moment could not fix with a name. We talked a little, and the link was mended. " I know who you are," I said to him. " You went in seventh wicket down for Harrow against Eton in fifty-dash, and made eighty-five not out I saw you.'9 Grey and severe, he took me for a kind of Cagliostro.

In my first summer quarter at the school, Montagu Butler was head-boy, and point in the eleven. Afterwards to be head-master for a good span of time, and then to follow worthily in the wake of scholars like Whewell and Thompson, in the unique post of Master of Trinity, Cambridge.. " Eheu fugaces, Postume! Postume!" No matter—it's a way they have. Five shillings, please! And one of my odd proud moments was when, many years afterwards, I found myself, much to my wonder—for such an unlicensed being —cheered on the old school steps as an eminent Harrovian, side by side with a con-temporary friend and new-made bishop, with whom I had driven down on Speech-day. "The dramatist and the bishop! The lion and the lamb!" as Butler said. But the bishop rather grumbled. He declared that he was only cheered professionally, while I got my tribute on my own account It was like a confused kind of dream appropriate to my strange Harrow life, unlike a boy's I think in many ways. For most of those Harrow days were dreamed away, except perhaps when the ***Merchant of Venice*** was enacted under my comic-acting-management.

Somewhere about sixteen I gave up being a small boy as altogether a mistake, and suddenly began to grow, outgrowing everything upon me, tails and all. I did it so fast and got so weak with it, that I was sent away to Sidmouth and Dawlish that I might perform the mango-trick on myself, apart from the observation of rude boys. I remember vividly a very Egyptian miracle of boils and blains that I passed through. They vanished, and the growth remained. Horizontally my figure then shot up. Times have now changed, and it moves in circles with me. It was a drawing-room figure once. Now it is a dining-room one.

CHAPTER XII

AT HARROW

I PAID one bitter penalty for being under-sized at Harrow, and have often wondered how much effect the incident had on my career. "Great effects of small causes" should be a good subject for a new philosopher's speculation. In due course, and rather fast, I had arrived at the upper-fifth form, which came in order first below the sixth, that Mount Olympus or high table of the school. Every week happened what was called the placing. According to his work during the seven days, each boy was seated in due order for the following week. In the upper-fifth the head-boy of the week was in himself a cynosure, in that he was seated in solitary state at a small side-table near the masters, the other boys ranged upon benches in the centre. I was proud of that post, and it gave me a stimulant I had never felt before, having been content with moderate successes that left me free to cultivate my own tastes, and I unwisely resolved to keep it all the time. But a catastrophe had occurred in the school. An upper boy had caned a lower boy by monitorial law; and the lower boy's parents raised an outcry. Richly the lower youth deserved it; but he was of noble origin, while the smiter was humble. So there were ructions, and they ended in the promotion in order of some of the bigger upper-boys of the fifth-form, to make an under-sixth, but sharing the upper-fifth class-room. I was passed over as too small, and after three days' glory marched out of my seat of honour, to be ranged upon those common benches while a big boy took my seat. Never shall 1 forget the burning sense of injustice which took possession of my soul. It is a feeling I have always deeply realised, on my own behalf and that of others, which is unworthy in a lawyer. But as a boy I felt it acutely. Why should I be publicly degraded as a scholar because I was small, and a big boy whom 1 didn't know had thrashed another one I didn't know either ? Thereon I registered a different vow, never to waste another hour that I could help on ancient scholarship; and it was a vow that more or less I fear I always kept The next week, in place of *being primus inter pares,* I came out number twenty-three in the reduced fifth form. When my days of close alliance with Dr. Vaughan arrived, I told him of my plight, and frank, if late, I remember, was his regretful acknowledgment of the wrong. He had kept some letters on the subject from my family, it appeared, who on this occasion seem to have been quite exceptionally active, consigned to a crowded pigeon-hole which, as he confessed to me with a chuckle, he labelled " Indignant Parents."

There was rather a small and silent circle of masters when first I went to Harrow, and prominent among the figures by the side of Billy Oxenham was Ben Drury, my own cousin of the scholar blood, whose Bennites for some reason were held in small consideration in the school. Wherefore I felt some satisfaction in being a Vaughanite in spite of kindred—apart from the obvious advantage of belonging to a race called after a surname instead of with undue baptismal familiarity, which none the less implied a pleasant sort of feeling for the masters who suggested it The tribal instinct prevailed in the young Vaughanites and Steelites—abbreviation in the Simmyites and Middlemites—Simpkin-sonians and Middlemisters being clearly impossible, and a grave reflection upon a master's personal semblance in the Monkey-ites. Ben Drury was a fine, courteous, and manly specimen, old school to the last degree, who wisely declined to encourage my youthful and sentimental attempts to make a kind of home-side in his house, and showed no preference for me over his other pupils, the boys at Vaughan's being distributed among different pupil-rooms for their private instruction out of school to safeguard head-magisterial dignity. New ideas were feeling their way to the birth at Harrow in my day which proved to be the beginning of changed phases of thought, and wider ideas of education. The modern side was soon to come to light, and my excellent friend of the earthquake and the apple to drop out of the running. Even as I should have found some difficulty in winning a German prize on such inadequate grounds not very long afterwards, it was, to say the least of it, incongruous that our French master should have been an Englishman of rather shallow French, and our mathematical teacher a Frenchman of very superficial English. Mathematiques he called his mystery, and in compliment to that and to his nationality, we knew him with some affectionate contempt for frog-land, as old Teek. His son, otherwise young Teek, was once captain of the eleven. He was tall and dark and sinuous, and very prehensile at long leg. But soon a whole wild horde of additional new masters descended on the school, which under Vaughan's rule was growing out of memory in numbers, whom we, the senior boys, when some of them came, regarded rather with patronage than with any other feeling. I remember one of them presuming to give me fifty lines to write out for something that offended him, and with a courtly bow—for I had grown up then—I replied that I must decline, and should refer him to the head-master. The head-master didn't like liberties being taken with his monitors and lieutenants, and treated Dominie junior to a severe lecture on the proprieties. Let us hope that he understood his place, as a master, better afterwards, My Gobbo days had past, and I was nothing if not the Doge,

Another of the junior masters imported in my day was Westcott, gentlest of scholars and sweetest-natured of men, lost to us as Bishop of Durham only the other day, a kind of replica of Dr. Vaughan, he always seemed to me. His very personality gave a meaning to the old expression for the classics—the Humaner Letters—while another churchman of the future came to Harrow at about the same period, in the person of Canon Farrar that was to be. His was a figure of a less convincing sort, and he came armed with methods which were to regenerate boy-kind, but didn't. In theory his course was noble. If the unregenerate one was accused of some breach of discipline, he was called upon to give his honour if he was guilty or not guilty. If he confessed, he was duly punished, otherwise his honour was accepted. And when with gentle mien and downcast eyes the future canon climbed the street that led to the school-gates, becapped and gowned and on his way to business, small boys would be seen clinging and trotting about his skirts and lavishly bestowing on him their thoughts as to everything that turned up. One little fellow cunning in the Farrar school, was brought before Ben Drury for some young offence, as caught in flagrant delict Brief and to the point, " Ben" told him to write out a hundred lines. The boy smiled a smile of compassion, and bowing, laid his hand upon his heart. " I give you my honour, sir," he said, "I was not there." Ben sat back in his chair, looked at the boy, and gasped: " *What ?* a boy's honour! What ? Write me out two hundred." Brutal, but not without philosophy. That boys will be boys and are, is as true as proverbs in general and truer; and a master has ever been a boy's fair game. Angels are not made out of school-boys, except in " Eric," and even in dawning manhood the more delicate virtues are not always sacred. It is in the latter stages of life, if any, that to have learned the ingenuous arts faithfully softens the manners and does not permit them to be wild. During the process, it has a tendency to make them wild rather than not. Such at least has been common experience during com-memorations and in lawless festivals in Tom Quad or Peckwater; and I count among my friends a scholarly tragedian, who, in the after days when Oxford boasted a the-atre, appeared then in a Shakespearean play, and a little tired the unsophisticated youth of Isis. Towards the end they became uproarious, and he addressed them in shrewd terms of rebuke. " I thought/' he said, "that in classic Oxford Shakespeare and myself would be safe in the hands of gentlemen/1 The appeal struck the wrong chord in the rising mind altogether, and shouts of delight greeted the tragedian. No, no I Yah-yah! Hear hear! Till one undergraduate more enterprising than the rest called out for silence, mounted the big drum in the orchestra, and made a speech. " Either this gentleman is a great tragedian as reported/' he concluded, "or he is not If he is, let us listen with respect If he isn't what on earth does he come here for ?M *Oh fortunati nimtum, sua si bona nbrint* What fun it all was, the salad-time, for in spite of the drawbacks of such mistaken training, Oxford was my emancipa-tion and my start

As there were no theatres then except the singular play-houses we constructed and acted in for ourselves—whereof more anon— we heckled wandering lectur-ers or entertainers who fell rashly into our hands. Chiefly in that connection do

I remember an excursion into electro-biology, a craze of the hour. A person of strong will caused a person of weak will to look fixedly at a brass disc in his hand until his will was absorbed. Whereon he believed and did everything he was told; if told he was a horse, he pawed the ground; if told to stand on one leg and support a chair on the other he did so. Our electro-biologist was a handsome young woman of a decided turn, and of the effective name of Eagle, who held undergraduates as dross. When one of her victims was pranc-ing horse-like on the platform, a sharp Oxonian asked him when he recovered: " What does a horse feel like ? " Before the applause that greeted the conundrum passed, " What does a boy feel like, sir ? Can you tell me ? " was the lady's counter. And the co-Oxonians, glorying in manhood, followed its instincts and sat upon the crushed. One result of that weird pythagore-an show was curious. We all of us wanted to test our powers of will, and to electro-biologise each other. So we bought discs and did—at Zoroastrian meetings, for the purpose held in our different Balliol rooms. Which was the weaker will and which the stronger was the problem, until it was proved by indisputable evidence, that whoever could most easily electro-biologise was likewise in his turn the most easily electro-biologisable. This led to confusion of wills, and so many animal shapes did we assume—or think we did—that our mystic meetings became a sort of Zoological carnival. I even remember one young man who had to explain that he had brayed, the particular utterance not having been generally recognised. But when we knew his animal we quite believed him. I confess that I cannot feel that the latter-day religious scientists have ever come near this earlier development of the unseen. In our young hands, and in ours alone, acting but as instruments of powers mysterious, has the Pythagorean soul taken a return ticket, and gone into a brute and back again without effect upon the principle of life.

Of some of our college-breakfasts over, the Dean of Chapel's head—a pleasant dark-blue link in the chain of memory having, as my readers will see, without effort connected Harrow-on-the-Hill with Balliol at the bottom of it—I discoursed out of due time in an earlier chapter of this work. That Dean of Chapel had a time with us, and in the after years was to suggest to me much harmless oddity of Oxford life, which in partnership with my wife—gifted with a keen woman's turn for story—I used in what turned into a popular comedy, called The Dan. It was enacted by that king of pure low-comedy and friend of many men, Johnnie Toole. The play, which first introduced Violet Vanbrugh — dear daughter of an early Devon friend—to London, is full of pleasant memories to us, darkened but by the constant pain of poor Toole's now cruel suffering and illness. He was difficult to manage, Toole; for " gagging " was his dream; and gagging, for the information of the uninitiate, means the improving of the author's language by the actor's own. In an earlier comedy of ours called *The Butler*, we gave him a free tongue. But in *The Don* we made a bold attempt to legitimise him, somewhat in vain, I fear. For Dons should never gag, though butlers may. Johnnie was rather awe-stricken at first, by such unwonted rise in social place, and he stuck to his text and behaved very well—for him—until he began to feel at home. After the play had been running for about a month I went into the dress-circle unbeknown, to watch, and he came on with a rather large red nose, though there was nothing bibulous about our Don whatever. Likewise he had, in course of part, to ask a languishing young widow how she had liked India. " It was very hot," she sighed, and the subject changed. But Johnnie had risen to the occasion then, and took her up. "Ah! that," he added, "was because of the pickles you ate." Nobody laughed. Such, my good friends, is gagging. Neither as author nor Oxonian did I quite approve. After the act I rushed round to his room and shook him. He had no idea that I was there, and apologised anxiously. " Got to be done, my dear fellow!" he said. " They expect it of me. I call it thickening the part" " Do you ?" quoth I. " I call it thinning the house." Johnnie was of manager-actors the kindliest, in never grudging laughs to any one. But it was not usual in his plays to have anything to laugh at, till he himself came on. When *The Butler* was first produced at Manchester, the opening scene between two of the characters caused, as it happened, a good deal of merriment at once. Toole heard the laughter in his room, and sent his dresser down, to ask, "what had gone wrong in front" Never was actor, in one sense, so amenable. Too amenable, by far. For at rehearsals, when he was not on the stage himself, he sidled off to his room to write several little letters, about nothing, leaving the author and the stage-manager to do the rest And always had to be summoned for his cue. One day in Newcastle, when we were rehearsing *The Don* with his company, he disappeared altogether, in the middle of the day, for the short luncheon interval. I was something of a martinet at rehearsals, as indeed with him one had to be. We waited to begin the scene, in vain. Half an hour passed —an hour—and still no Toole. We fretted, waited, looked at our watches, till at last I took it on myself to dismiss the rehearsal. Toole must have been called away on pressing business. My wife and I strolled homewards to our lodging, and three streets off met Toole, careless and happy, arm-in-arm with his ***tidus Achates and*** nurser-in-general, excellent George Loveday. He had no idea of the time, and simply gasped when I told him what I had done. The dear old fellow had been in the flower-market, buying for my wife the choicest nosegay he could find. That was the man, on both sides, and at once. Only the other day my wife and I met him once again at Brighton in his bath-chair—as he is now. For some five minutes we talked quite cheerily about the past. Then he broke down, and I left him—for all memory of us seemed gone. It wasn't, for at the hotel where we were staying, my wife received from him that evening a beautiful bouquet of flowers. Upon our wedding-day, twenty-three years before—of which we didn't even think he knew more than of her address—he had sent her in the early morning the bridal flowers she carried. Such thoughts live.

I shall not forget reading ***The Don*** to him and Loveday first, in the Old Ship at Brighton this time. For he was a wandering star, whose author wandered with him, keeping guard. Loveday and I were in a deep conspiracy together over ***The Don***, having carefully concealed from Toole the fact that we meant to risk him, for the first time for years, in a higher class of comedy altogether. " Now listen," Loveday, who knew the play, said, " this will frighten him out of his wits, to start with, and when you've finished, it will take me a week to persuade him to do it. Then it will be all right, so don't mind/' And so I read. Loveday in an arm-chair, chuckling; Toole on a sofa, silent and absorbed. After the first act he seemed so meditative, and smileless, that I secretly asked Loveday what on earth he was thinking about. " All right," was the answer. "He likes it He's thinking about his gags.1 Then came a scene for the scoot or gyp— called skip, as I wanted to mix the universities —that well-known male appendage of the two. When I had finished it, Toole spake at last. "I suppose, Herman," he remarked, "that that is to be Emily Thome's part" For an act and a half, he had taken my scout to be an old woman; and I thought that I had read so well.

Oxford to the rescue, for later tragedies take one off the line. So thoroughly had my last Harrow six months, under the torturing personal care of the most finished of all the classical scholars I have ever known, in his beloved Greek especially—head-master and best friend in spite of that anti-classic resolu-tion of mine—set me up, so to speak, in die best Greek poets and prosists, that I fear I practically lived on my little capital as a spendthrift ever afterwards. Dr. Vaughan was not much at-tracted by divine philosophy, I fear. Neither was I. We have it on Milton's author-ity that only fools can think it harsh and crabbed. Therefore I was a fool, for I did so do, which only means that tastes must differ after all. Indeed no crab, however backward in his walks abroad, struck me as to compare for pace and claw with him whom we called the Staggerist Whenever I struggled with the involved periods of Aristotle, and vainly strove after the smallest interest in the powers and energies of the apolaustic man, I used re-belliously to reflect that, with a little more of Vaughan, I could have written better Greek myself. As for Plato, heaven forgive me, he used to strike me as a writer of pretty children's books with a carefully transparent style, which ought to have been illustrated with pretty pictures to carry the illusion out The Socratic method offended my sense of justice, and of logic too. I didn't believe, being still young and always imaginative, in the dummies whom Socrates stuck up only to knock them down, with long conundrums leading to no answer whatso-ever. It was like a dead shot popping at the Aunt Sallies in a French booth, and most unfair. When one of the most monstrous of those Tales of a Tormentor ended, I felt inclined to call out, with the small boy when he was told of Jonah and the whale, or Professor Huxley confronted with his favourite bug-bear, the Herd of Swine—" I don't believe that story."

Hence it was that that rebel-resolve against the classics, in abeyance during my Vaughan half-year, came to the front again. Twice I tried for the Balliol scholarship. The first time from Harrow, though as usual a year too soon. But I ran near enough to winning it to be admitted to the college without the ordeal of being examined for mtriculation. In the next season I tried for it again, being then a first year Balliol man. The spare autumn between Harrow and Oxford I had spent under a reverend private tutor in South Wales among the pools and mosses of the Wye, which at-tracted me more than my books ; and as the temporary guardian of my mind was careless if it improved or not, it didn't. So from my second essay for the Balliol ribbon, I emerged in the ruck not anywhere at all. But for all that the charm of my classic favourites and Vaughan's, Æschylus and Aristophanes and gossip Herodotus, and Homer the apocryphal,

and, on the Latin side, fiery Juvenal, and take-to-bed Horace, and the gende Virgil, abided always, and abides even now. I cannot profess to give any reason whatever for holding, that they refined and moulded in some unknown way my inborn love of English letters. But I am quite sure they did, and deeply do I thank my doctor, and those dead teachers for it

CHAPTER XIII

ON MEN OF BALLIOL AND OTHER THINGS,

WITH SIDE-LIGHTS UPON JOWETT

BALLIOL COLLEGE, the famous creation of John de Balliol and Devorguilla his wife, was in a high state of prosperity in the days when I was first numbered amongst her children,

Proud in the beauty of her matchless charms, Supreme in science, and supreme in arms,

—a couplet which still remains on my ear as the opening of a Harrow prize poem of Montague Butler's on the subject of Athens. She had certainly won herself a notable position at Oxford. She played fine cricket, and shone conspicuous at the head of the riven She was displeased with herself if she monopolised less than half of the first class in the schools; she took in prizes and medals as largely as she sent out Fellows to mould half the other colleges of Oxford My three surviving links with the University are all heads of their various colleges now—Lincoln and Exeter and Oriel—and all these were Balliol men of my time. The first of them was an especial ally of mine when we were there, and being just as much my senior as the relation required, officiated for me one summer as my tutor, with a reading-party in the English lakes, upon the plain of reedy Grasmere. I sup-pose we read I am quite sure that we played, and both of us being full of fun and of high spirits, though my own were always subject to eccentricities of mood and relapses into solitude, we estab-lished quite a new lake-school in our way between us. The coincidence of name be-tween Merry and Merivale was a windfall for the local wags, and by dint of pleasant introductions, most of them of our own audacious contriving, we found ourselves at home in various pleasant circles of the place. Very nice parents introduced us to very nice girls; and that attractive class of humanity—which, as far as I can judge, has, in spite of the wisdoms, never been much improved upon—was known to us both by the pleasant and familiar style of " the Maries." We got on with the Maries very well, and rowed them on the lake in the afternoons, or listened to them sing-ing in the evenings, and did not—from the point of view of life-experience—lose as much time as perchance we did in other ways. In our segregate male-hours, when books were closed, we swam in the lake, or played yard-cricket with balls of india-rubber against the door of our little tenement, rented close upon the water for our vacation-space. Or we had long afternoons of climb on the surrounding hills and fells, under the energetic guidanceof the responsible chief of our party—we were five in all—one of the college tutors, affectionately known as Jemmy Riddell—climbs which from an inborn and unconquerable dislike for walking exercise I was wont to shirk when possible, preferring, where tennis and rackets were not, to moon or boat about the lake, not unfrequently in Merry's congenial company. We liked to sit upon a sloping height and hurl huge stones into the lake below, which we called corriging. And one day when he had gained a higher level than I, and I was lying luxurious on my back, I felt a hurtle in the air and raised my head, to find it narrowly shaved by a large flying boulder. My friend had nearly cor-riged me on the skull, and brought this veracious history to a premature end It was dangerous, no doubt, but better than walking with an object If the object is not to be otherwise attained, why not drop it ? The great lake feature of that year was a comet And it was one whereof the Ettrick shepherd might have been thinking when he sang:

Oh, on thy sparkling prow to ride, To cleave the depths of heaven with thee!
And plough the twinkling stars aside, Like foam-bells on a tranquil sea.

I am inclined to think that Riddell's finished scholarship had much to do with Balliol's success. Scott was the master of my day; Jowett its more famous tutor. No character that has attained to equal eminence in my time ever more completely puzzled me. Never has a great reputation been to me more of a bewilderment. The lovable nature of the man was always with him, and a pleasant attraction to his young pupils and associates. Though not by office my tutor, he showed me great personal kindness and attention, almost after the manner of Dr. Vaughan, and took me for many walks with him, my objections to the exercise having to suppress themselves for those occasions. There never was so silent a companion, or one, I am bound to say, with less that I could ever discover of the sense of humour with which he was always credited. The quaint sayings recorded of him were quaint in sheer unconsciousness, such as his famous remark to the stern Chancellor and his myrmidons who waited for him to sign the Thirty-Nine Articles as Greek Professor, when he was suspected of combustible heresy in common with the present Archbishop of Canterbury, of all men, for so do even heresies pass away. " Will you not sign the articles, sir ? " as Jowett stood unmoved before them. He looked prepared for martyrdom and they for action. But after a little pause he put his head on one side, and in the cherubic treble that matched the cherubic face, he said: " Yes, if you'll give me a pen."

He was always putting his head on one side, and humming to himself, in place of conversation. As silence, I am afraid, has never been my failing, he was fond of letting me wander on to him about book-fancies and imaginations and anything in my head, listening always with a kind of composed smile settled at one corner of his mouth, as who should say, " I could an if I would, but won't" He listened, for if I stopped he drew me out with some short question or another. But he never would add anything. Sometimes he volunteered some strange remark, as when once he stayed me on our walk, and said: " I can't quite make you out. I think your mind stops somewhere." I wonder if that is how men gain credit for profundity. I could attach no meaning to that theory, and cannot now. All that I could answer was, " I don't know. I suppose so. I find it stopping in all sorts of places." Was Jowett occupied in building up out of my personality a theologic theory of man of the kind so supposed to occupy him ? One thing I will say, that in all my experience and knowledge of him I never knew him utter one syllable or suggest one thought which could disturb the faith and contentment of any man. Nor do I believe he ever did. Theological discussions have not been in my line. Perhaps my life, at that date, was too careless to leave room for any interest in doubts. But I know of instances in which more inquiring friends of mine tried anxiously to draw him out upon such topics, and were quietly but firmly discouraged. Jowett's own faith, I must frankly say, seems to me, from the evidence before the world, and from all that is known of him, to have been in a pure state of doctrinal solution from first to last His heresies, if such they were, were founded upon shifting but very gentle sand. He had deep faith in goodness and in kindness, and, in true Christian spirit, he practised it in his life. But to put him or his sermons and essays into any recognised category at all is, in my judgment, idle. He was not even a broad Churchman in the sense of Dean Stanley.

My walks with him were not as my walks with Vaughan. In that dear master's overflowing talk — abundant humour, delicate scholarship — I found a fund of teaching, which, to do myself justice, I have always loved to turn to my advantage from elder and congenial minds. It was a far greater treat to me to listen to him than to talk to Jowett, as was expected of me. Once I grew fairly tired of such enforcement and took revenge. We started on our walk, and I said nothing. A mile went by—two miles—I didn't speak. Jowett began to fidget, whistle, look at meat an early stage upon that silent promenade. At last he couldn't bear it, stopped in the walk, and addressed me with : " Won't you say something ? " But I was obstinate, and said it was quite time that he began.

How much of Jowett's fame came of his gift for saying nothing is not for me to say. He was a good man, as I knew him, if there has been one in his kind. I have not cared to inquire about him more. But I fear that he a little loved to make sport with me for Philistines. I was, if I may say so, rather a favourite plaything with him. He was fond of me, I think; but he declined to take me seriously. When afterwards he heard that I had written a tragedy he didn't believe it. With Swinburne—a Balliol contemporary-— it was quite another thing, and as it should be. Jowett—be it whispered, and very much to his credit — obstinate college-bachelor though he was, was by no means above an amiable weakness for the Maries. Maries matured, no doubt. But Maries. He loved to have little breakfast-parties for ladies from London. And he liked to ask me to meet them. At one such feast he put me to a cruel trial. It was a dull party, and nobody said much. I felt uncomfortable in so much silent splendour, and was thinking of a tennis match I was to play that day. Suddenly, and in an awful pause, he set his head—may I say cocked it?—in the usual place, and looked at me. And without any preamble observed : " Merivale is a man who looks at everything from a Shakespearean point of view." All the double-glasses went up icily, and I nearly sank through the floor. I was not among his guests at his famous under-graduate breakfast, when nobody said anything all the time. When the hour came he opened the door and said: " Good-morning, gentlemen; cultivate the art of conversa-tion." Casual as they seemed, the spasmodic Lake teachings of my colleague Merry did my modest classical aspirations more good than those of anybody else ever did, Vaughan excepted Bright and light and practically of my own years, he read with me more on the footing of a fellow student than a tutor, and had the gift of understanding his man, a matter over which the authorised tutor troubles himself but little. He carries his bed of Procrustes about him by way of a curricle, and jams his pupils in or pulls them out for the length of it, regardless of the size or make of their mental bonework. For a time I studied, in a sudden rush of desire for depth, under the eminent judge and amateur prize-fighter that was to be, of whose breakfast over the decanal head I discoursed before. He was a great scholar, but, O Lord, how dull! I would as lief have sat at the feet of Aristotle himself, or of the complicated historian known to our youth as Thick-sides, from his dyspeptic pastry of obscure diction. "D'abord de la clarté, puis de la clarté, et toujours de la clarté!" said Anatole France when somebody asked him the receipt for writing to be read. But the worship of the obscure remains what it always was, seeing that it makes a man look so clever—to the mass who feel obliged to take him at his own valuation—to profess to understand that which cannot be understanded. Ask him to explain, and it's a different thing. It's the contemptuous but facile answer of, "Why, good heavens! don't you see?" You don't; but you fear to be called stupid, and you pretend you do. The Thucydideans and the Aristotelians must have been the Carlylese and Browningites of their day. For those two authors, even as these two, had much that was well worth saying to say, but they either couldn't or wouldn't take the trouble to say it in plain Greek. So the usual host of witless imitators saw their chance, and imitated all the masters' obscurity without acquiring any of their meaning. Once in the summer-shades of Surrey I discussed Browning with a famous sculptor-author, and stuck to my favourite text that our share of time is too small to allow us to read our own tongue with a dictionary, and that an author who won't take the pains to be readable as well as wise ought not to print at all. He inveighed against my ignorance, maintaining Browning to be like a stream of crystal to those who had souls of sympathy. So I took up a volume of Browning and read him a passage of blank verse with all due emphasis, then asked him if he honestly understood it. He shrugged the shoulder of superiority, and, smiling, put the question by, like the gentleman in Tennyson. Of course he did, but couldn't help me if I didn't. Well, I did not, and said so. I had read out the passage in an inverted form, from the bottom of the page upwards. Literary affec-tation is a dreadful thing. Bulwer Lytton, as we know, is as a name of scorn to the superior persons who never read him, but apparently only read each other. But a pithy sentence of his Sir John Vesey's constantly recurs to me about it, as a small picture of whole waggonloads of letters. " All humbug—humbug upon my soul!"

So, then, it fell out that the coming judge was deep, but likewise obscure and dull. That was as it should be, for he was born to deliver judgments and keep costs and appeals going. Yet, as I have said, he had in his way grim humours of his own, but thought himself bound to keep them out of business. During another long vacation—and my first —I went for some weeks to be tutored— good heavens! the number of them we all have, as if continuity of mind were in itself as nothing!—down on the shore of the beautiful estuary which lies between Barmouth and Dolgelly. There was this wild confusion of instruction duly made worse confounded. My new classic was a Jelf, and a ripe scholar too. But he was, of course, unlike his predecessors, as two loving Merrys are not moulded on one stem. He was quite sternly funless in his Greek and Latin, and after the few weeks of highly paid—on my side— intercourse allowed us, we naturally parted on a mutual footing of respect and misunderstanding. I had no time to get at him, nor he at me. In my own way the while I pursued my own English studies for myself, and in his well-stocked library, reading all round, in verse and prose, whatever held my interest, from chronicle to novel, and ever ensuing my own yearning text of style—" De la clarté, de la clarté, toujours de la clarté!" For so, and so alone, the truest training ever will go on, under the law of individual gift-

Es bildet ein Talent sich in der Stillc
Sich ein Charakter in den Strom der Welt

If I was in the clouds more or less, as I always am and must be, I am not sorry for it, though where the main chance is concerned my clouds have been mighty thick and thun-derous. I can never suspect that I am being taken in, therefore I always am. It is an unsafe residence, cloudland, but it is very sweet And one of my various reasons both for personal liking and art-appreciation of that most imaginative of Shakespeare's actors—Beer-bohm Tree—is that he wrote me all unknowing, once, one of those little sentences which make for mental righteousness: " To live in the clouds is just to live in heaven." More power to Cloudland. I agree with him. What says sweet Schiller's Zeus to the poet-artist, who asks for a little something, after the traders and the lawyers have done all the grabbing ?

Was than ? spricht Zeus—die Welt ist weggegeben, Der Herbst, die Jagd, der Markt ist nich mehr mein:

Willst du in meinem Himmel mit mir leben,
So oft du kommst, er soil dir offen sein.

Like all true cloudlanders, at that appro-priate age, even as more or less even by conjugal licence ever since, I was always falling in love at first sight and out again. The object, I must say, was always equally prepared for both. It was six to one and half a dozen of the other. We did each other no harm. My love-letters, I verily believe, would make the fortune of several professors of that of late resuscitated art. I was accused of being fond of flirting. I was not. I was fond of being in love, I confess. In love with all lovable women, all at once I feel. like Johnnie Toole, that it is expected of me. Three pupils were we at Jelfs, and we all fell in love with one and the same Mary. Yet she was one of three sisters, and it was unfair on the others, as she was the least clever of the three. But then she took the liberty of being the prettiest, even to distraction's verge, though all were comely and of feminine presence. We three young men disputed that maiden's favours by all fair means, and as their father rented a cottage from our tutor in the grounds, used to court admission into his circle in divers ways. At last I tried means I feel to have been unfair. It was arranged one day that we three Horatii "should walk up Cader Idris and leave the three Curiatiae alone for once. When the time came I feigned indisposition, due partly to love and partly to walkophobia. After a close morning's study I sought out that cottage, manoeuvred for an invitation to luncheon, and, favoured by friendly sisters, secured a whole delicious afternoon with the object, all to myself! When late in the evening the two climbers returned and heard of my successful turpitude there was almost a duel. The youngest of us three was quite a boy, not yet at college. But the elder was well my senior, a Christ Church man of proof He came into my room just as I was going to bed, and, having picked a quarrel on some fictitious ground, white with wrath and nightgown, he waved his good right arm at me and said : " Sir, henceforth we meet no more as friends but as foes!" As I hope for forgiveness, he used those very words. Shaken with mute laughter, I sustained the shock, and have ever since wondered if, after all, melodrama is not the truest language of instinctive passion.

When that mixed period of study reached its end, after we had vied in prodigies of valour under the fair one's eyes, casting off our coats and swimming across armlets of the estuary with fishing-tackle in our mouths, where as a matter of fact we could have walked round to as much purpose, and in much less time—and otherwise fooling as divine youth can fool—we elders went upon our Oxford way, and the cadet remained as pupil. I think I was the favourite up to that But such good use did he make of his chances afterwards that, young as he was, he wooed and won the beauty, who afterwards became his wife. It was a romance of real devotion, and a sad one, on which I have no need to dwell. She was a very young wife when she died, but after-fidelity has not often been more steadfast than was his.

But one strange incident attached to the episode for me. The youngest of those three girls was very young, awkward and shy, but curiously clever. I found that out by accident towards the end of the time, and it had an odd effect upon my inconstant mind. Shall it be confessed that I was seized with strange misgivings as to whether, after all, I had not been smitten by the wrong Curiatia? I had but just the time to suspect, in this my new discovery, a vein of originality of a very rare kind. So much was I intrigued that I con fided to my senior friend—the imminent and deadly breach between us having been by some means healed over—that the young girl had a great deal in her somewhere and was bound to become somebody. I have never met her again from that time to this, nor has communication of any kind passed between us. I don't suppose she remembers my name from Adam's, whatever his family appellation may have been. Perhaps it was Tree, like Beerbohm's, so that my dreamland actor may claim a more direct descent from our perplexing common parents than the rest of us. But it has been my odd lot to be mixed up, at some time and in some way or another, with half the celebrities of all sorts that trot the patient globe. And I shall not forget the thrill of sympathetic interest with which I read of the sudden and striking success in literary fields of my original little friend of the Barmouth Estuary, Rhoda Broughton, with a sort of sense of proprietorship missed. I have never since been able to lose my watchful pleasure in her career.

So in my Oxford journey the shadow of Cader Idris faded from my path, and many years afterwards I saw it only that once again. Even as before in youth, I,steadily refused to climb it, but revisited the estuary coast and fed on recollection. Strange—so strange!

> The lapping waters danced and bore
> The bark of Memory to the shore,
> And overwrought with cares of man,
> I lived in boyhood once again.

Excuse a habit of improvising a quotation when I haven't got one handy, after the convenient precedent of great Scott when he referred his sudden couplets to head a chapter withal to the elastic authority of Old Play.

After my wandering, hopeless method, Cader Idris, having got me in her grip, insists upon recalling Henry Merrywether, the wittiest lawyer of my time, to me. Oh that the judges wouldn't joke so much! Everybody has to laugh whenever they do it, badly or indifferently, with the helpless and heartbroke litigants haunting for indefinite hours the Halls of the lost Footsteps miscalled the Courts of Justice. In all Sir Mountstuart Grant Duffs kindly diaries I have met with but one severe allusion. He found himself among a nest of judges telling comic tales. And every single tale, he says, turned upon some funny miscarriage of plain justice. He went home sad and heart-sick like the poor suitors. Even a great Justice has been found to say, with a laugh, of late, that his court of King's Bench had nothing to do with honour and morality. A heart-breaking admission from such a source. Merrywether was a stout man amongst the stout, and when term came he was once greeted by the then Lord Chancellor with delicate bigwig courtesy. " Upon my word, Merrywether, you are growing as fat as a porpoise." Whereat he bowed and said: " The nearer, my Lord, to the great Seal." Once a fussy dullard complained to him that he was going to take a few days holiday in Wales, wanted to do Snowdon and Cader Idris both, and didn't know how to combine them. " Easy enough," was the answer. " Go up Snowdon, and down Cader Idris." Whereat the man sate down to think it out, like the people who searched for an answer to Shirley Brooks's conundrum, "Sydney Smith said to Horace Walpole, 'How is it that you are so fond of green vegetables, although you live at Twickenham ?' Horace smiled at the jest, but never forgave the sarcasm." Once Merry wether went to hear Albert Smith's *Ascent of Mont Blanc,* and at the box-office found that there was but one seat left in the stalls. Another man was just before him, doubting between that and the gallery. " I should go into the gallery if I were you," suggested Merrywether, "because it's nearer the summit." The man took the hint and the wit took the stall. He was a prosperous Parliamentary Q.C., and when somebody asked him to what especia' qualities he attributed his great success at the Bar he simply said: " To three of them : Unbounded impudence, popular manners, and total ignorance of law

CHAPTER XIV

so?

IF the romance of my North-Welsh long vacation was Love, that of my South-German was, as I well remember, Prison. Tutor-less this time, a friend of mine and I departed on the quest of knowledge together, and chose as our headquarters the Florence of the North, the good city of Dresden. Nobody who only knows united Germany since, on the strength of her big war, she has grown so desperately exacting and cross and quarrelsome, can realise how pleasant a sojourn disunited Germany was. The little Courts gave all their towns a flavour of good society. Nobody could be nicer than the Saxons except the Hanoverians, or the Bavarians than either.

> Und so sagt man das in Sachsen
> Stets die häbschen Mädchen wachsen—
> Sagt sie—Ei? ich ***denke schien***
> Kann ganz allein nach Haäse ***giehn***—
> Dresden ist doch sehr gemäthlich,
> st so sehr gemäthlich !

So was the Saxon ancient quizzed in the famous Faust words in the great burlesque play of the day—curiously like a kind of ***Belle of New York*** by anticipation in scheme, though in execution an artistic show instead of mere buffoonery—known as ***Flick and Flock,*** being the strange adventures of two wonderful heroes who went everywhere and did everything. Dances and songs and capital comic acting made the play exceedingly bright, and the personality of the English travelling peer, Lord Mixpikel by name and style, who was the most amusing specimen of the imperturbable " Briton" mit der spleen—the liberal German equivalent avoided for pleasantness—I ever saw upon the stage, dwells ever among my Reisebilder, my Heine-named Pictures of Travel. Shipwrecked and at the bottom of the sea, yet with tall hat and tight frock-coat quite unruffled, he was received with hostile demonstrations by King Neptune, whowagged his beard and shook his trident at the in-truder and threatened him in violent submarine. "Wer ist der Mann mit der Gabel?" said Mixpikel to his companions in trouble, quite unmoved and in his best German : "Who is the man with the fork ? I haven't been introduced to him." And great was the delight when the play ended with a series of panoramic views of the European capitals, London coming last. The different atmospheric effects of the climates had all been cleverly reproduced, but our own ozonic city figured as one large yellow blotch. "You needn't spend much time in seeing London," observed the personally conducting gnome. "It's all in that" Brave, jolly student-days! I felt myself quite a Bursch as I smoked my Heidelberg pipe and drank my Lager beer on the Bruhl Terrace or among the Alleys —not of the kind affected of Sally, but miniature tree-lined boulevards—and listened or joined in as the ditties were trolled out:

> Das macht mir alles
> ein, Hab' ich gelt,
> hab ich kein!
> Hab' ich gelt, trink' ich Rudesheimer,
> Hab' ich kein, trink' ich Pompenheimer!
> Das macht mir alles ein,
> Hab' ich gelt, hab' ich kein!

Oh inimitable lyric spirit of Teutonic land! No man in that delicious sphere shall vie with you for pathos or for humour either. It seems so strange that it should be so! For purposes of speech, no effort softens the harshness of the tongue away, infinitely softer though it was, of course, in the Saxon mouth than in the rough gul-lets of Berlin. Even for purposes of music, great as in that province also Germany has been, I am always wishing that in the matter of words they would reduce all things alike to Music's native tongue—Italian—as in the days or nights when Covent Gar-den was a Royal Italian Opera indeed, instead of a kind of Babel with pretensions to strange things in Depth, quite unjustified by directors or stage-managers. " Poly-glott House " should be inscribed above its portals now. But where is the use of

> Urn stets heute und gläcklich zu leben,

Will ich, Freunde, die Lehre euch geben.
after—

Il segreto per esser felice,
So per prova, einsegnogli amici !

Yet in blank verse Germany can hold her own as a good second to the Anglo-Saxon, and syllable for syllable almost at times. Through the kindred nature of the tongues is Shakespeare reproduced by Schlegel. One line occurs to me still, as I remember it first striking on my ear when Dawisen and Uhlrich played Benedick and Beatrice that distant summer, in that head-centre of stage art in those days, the Dresden Theatre,

Rinnt nicht dies Sprach wie Eisen durch dein Blut
was moulded on one stem indeed with
Runs not this speech like iron through your blood?

It is in the Lyric, the daintiest and most sensuous of all poetic forms, that Germany takes highest honours in the divine schools of art; and it has always seemed to me un-explainable why. One would have thought that the graces and daintinesses of speech would be more needed for that form than any other. But where Shakespeare was near his greatest the Germans have been greater.

Heine and Ubland are kings among the pure lyrists ; and the Rhine traveller who, in spite of tunnels and steam-cries, still dreams of legend as he passes the Loreley rock, forgets, if he ever knew, that not only the garland of verse that circles the soul-less waterwitch,
    A fair and wondrous maiden
    On those same rocks behold;
    The gems that she wears are golden,
    The hair she combs is of gold.
    With comb that is golden she combs it,
    And sings her song thereby,

That breathes to a wild weird burden,
A wonderful melody—

that not only the garland, I say, but the very legend itself, which seems so immemorial, are the invention of Heine. The rivers and forests of Germany teem with legendary verse, old Barbarossa and the rest included, while as for the ditties of good fellowship and friendship she has nowhere a fellow. Who that has clinked the farewell glass in some homely German circle can forget the round—

Liebe—lebe—scherze—schwurme—
Ich erfreue mich mit dir!
Härme mich, als ich dich harme,
Ufld sei wieder from mit mir ?

But really I must put the Muse into blinkers here. Germany, on the literary side, always has upon me the effect which Mrs. Alfred Wigan told me brandy-and-water had upon her. It makes me want to sing. On the political side, it doesn't

The Dresden Theatre of that day was a delightful institution. For three nights in the week Music reigned in the graceful and well-proportioned house like a larger Haymarket— long since gone to the flame-god, who claims most of them in the end—sweeping in a perfect semicircle round the open centre of the great place, hard by the bridge whereby hanged my prison tale, and by the eager river. Sometimes it was a feast of frolic, like **Flick und Flock,** but oftener the tuneful favourites of that day, impartially from the three great music-lands, Italy, Germany, and France, but all in German text There is no harm in translations of the best foreign operas, when, as in those countries, home-production is the staple. But in a country where there would seem to have been no opera-composers but Balfe and Wallace, and no operas left of them but the **Bohemian Girl** and **Maritana,** the less we talk about our musical genius the better. We knight the smallest specimens we find for leading bands and playing waltzes, if for nothing else, but that is about all And it is futile to make spasmodic efforts after a national opera when there are only translations to build it up with. An opera-house without operas should be but a Hibernian dream. But we are immensely pleased with our musical attainments, and we do talk. And, after all, Balfe and Wallace were but watery imitations of Auber. Gilbert and Sullivan, in their delightful partnership, came nearer absolute originality in music than any others we have had. There is no echo in them whatsoever of the ordinary opera bouffe which reached its highest water-mark in Offenbach. And one of their series, *The Yeomen of the Guard,* has appealed to me always as comic opera pure and simple and of no mean order either.

But I am outside my rights in venturing on music I am not as badly off as Dean Stanley, who knew but two tunes, one which was " God save the Queen " and the other which wasn't Where I can love music, I can love it deeply, and am eclectic enough to be touched to the heart by the lilt of a melodious ballad, or fascinated altogether by the instrumental magic of a Tannkäuser or a Valkyrian ride. Otherwise I am but as a dunce upon the matter, and cannot but hold that, where the Muses number nine the votaries of Our Lady of the Quavers take far too much unto themselves. And, after all, most music is so very bad. I hope that I have it in my soul, after Shakespeare's ostracism of those that haven't But all of it, I can't. And I am ever haunted by a weak suspicion that, after all, the rapture which Music causes is out of all due proportion to the agony that it inflicts. Oh those musical afternoons in a close drawing-room, with lithe cups of tea and cakes between, and the hollow murmurs after each little half-baked warble, " Thank you, so very nice!" Oh those tutelary scales on the other side of a party-wall, even where the scaly one is an expert! Oh those bands of wandering brass, so like to public speaking of a certain kind! And oh, above all, those organs of barrel, which the populace so love, that to claim musical instincts for them is but a mockery. I wonder if the average Briton's adoration of a barrel-organ springs from the same source as his worship of a Lord, an undistinguishing love of handles for their own sake ? Much humbug on the loose, you know, and everywhere.

The plays at Dresden found me more at home. It was a wonderful company there, that of the early sixties. Two tragedians at the head not to be easily bettered, a striking contrast to each other. Dawisen, ugly and rough, the George Frederick Cooke of Germany, but full of strange power and grim sardonic humour. And Email

Devrient, old then, no doubt, but Kemble-like in form and grace and style, though a far greater master in the natural than they. His Hamlet was the princeliest I have ever seen, so from one side the best. It may seem an odd thing to say, but I have been reminded of it most because for that same specialty, by a Hamlet of our own unknown to general fame, an actor lately lost to us, James Nutcombe Gould. He was handsome, refined, and princely to the core ; but as I have before spoken of his father's remarkable talents for acting, and claimed him as a kinsman of my own, it is not for me to raise a charge of prejudice. But it is curious that, learning from his father, he had acquired much both of the virtues and the faults of the old style of elocution. To me, it is a pleasure to hear the lines of Shakespeare for their own sake, when well and truly spoken, even with less of mind than Gould's to back them. Dawisen struck me most in Shylock and in Benedick. For the first he made no effort to raise sympathy, but played him as a savage, grim and avaricious, who had lived on for money's sake alone till, through whatever words, he owned no God but that, Christian or Hebrew. The true Shylock to my own mind, and clear in every line. Mammon does claim his worshippers like that. Dawisen's Benedick was a most quaint conception. He was a rough soldier of fortune out of his element, amusedly puzzled by the fine company he got into, making the jests of a Diogenes or a Timon on humankind as he saw it, useful for his sword alone and feeling it, disliking women heartily from a mistrust of his own ill-favoured phiz, and at first bothered, then boyishly delighted, at the idea of a girl like Beatrice falling in love with such as him. And such a Beatrice as Fraälein Ulrich, too, fair and tall, young, and straight as an arrow. All restlessness, caprice, and an ungoverned charm. Hot head and warmer heart; delightful altogether—really attracted by the ugly cynic from the first, in spite of herself and all her training. Ulrich was but a young girl just beginning then. It was no surprise to me to learn that she developed, afterwards, into one of the greatest actresses in Germany. One of the smaller details which struck me at the time—and the German artists have been often provided with a very special gift of insight into Shakespearean effect—was her first entrance in a riding habit as if fresh from horseback, a glow of exercise upon her face and in her manner, and a jewel-headed whip tapping the tiny boot impatiently. It seemed so exactly Beatrice, so fit an entrance on the scene of the imperious Lady Disdain ! The Dresden troop was worthy of its chiefs but it is only the chiefs whom one wishes to recall. The scythe of Time must mow the rest away. Devrient and Dawisen seldom played together, for the policy of two stars in one sphere was never good for managerial commerce long. The star-gazers grow accus tomed to more than one light for their money, and stop at home for the next constellation. But that was a memorable pair, was Dawisen Mephisto and Devrient Faust, with poetic Ulrich for their Goethe Marguerite. One of our many inartistic English blunders has been that, as far as I know, the regular acting version of Goethe's Faust has never been translated for the English stage. Yet it is standard as ***Hamlet*** is with us. We have had the comic fiend of melodrama disguised in every form—of opera or ballet, spectacle or pantomime—but never the real thing. Yet it was to me an interesting reality. I haunted the Dresden theatre upon every play-night On opera-nights, if I was not tempted, there were the summer breezes on the Bruhl Terrace overlooking Elbe, with Dresden beyond-river, and its balmy pleasure gardens twinkling like diamonds in the dying heat By day, the working hours apart, there were the wanderings through the avenues of the town, the friendly palavers with the young attachés of the Legation, the kindly welcome in two or three Saxon homes where I had introductions, the boat trips up-stream to the factory of Meisen, where Dresden of the cross-swords tempted us with all her china, or, by a little more of water-way, a plunge into the miniature mountain-scenes of Saxon Switzerland. There were the historic curios of the famed Green Vaults; there was the mighty and mov-ing Mass, with the full band, in the Roman Catholic Head Church of the little protesting state; and, above and beyond all, at every odd hour tobe frequented always, the gallery of galleries, which was my first serious introduction to the wide world of painting. Have I said that I was given to much falling into love ? Indeed, I did it there, and once for all Through all the changes and charms of this mortal art, through all the churches and galleries of Madrid and Seville, of Florence and of Rome; through the long miles of Louvre treasures and the fog-brown glooms of our own national gallery; through Titian's and Tintoret's haunts in mournful Venice; through sculpture as through painting, and by the three Venuses one by one, the Capitol, the Medici, the Milo; through all the Titan power of Michael Angelo; through all the daring realism of Velasquez ; through Andrea del Sarto's incomparable tenderness and Fra Angelica's monastic fervour; through the quaint angularities and humour of the Flemish school, I have been haunted, always and for ever, by the memory of one pictured face, as first it broke upon my young ignorance in the shrine-room set apart for it, throned as it should be, divine and all alone. The face of the Sistine Madonna, with that strange, unutterable, unearthly expression of a rapt and solemn awe—the awe of nothing but a chubby baby face, which none the less suggests behind it some supernatural trace of whence it came, made her my mistress in the Arts at once. I can no other. I am mightily pleased to know that my taste was So closely shared by a brilliant young painter, who in his buoyant letters from Rome could sing of nothing to his friends save the glories of Raphael, though I part company with him altogether in his depreciation of the might of Michael Angelo. He didn't like the massive, and I love it upon other lines. Taking my wife to Rome after a passage of twenty years, I recognised in the street at once the Church of St Peter in the Chains which holds the Moses, and led her straight, under the guidance of memory, to the corner in which he stands. Even for Raphael I would not stain my worship of the Titian. Otherwise I was always of Mr. Clive Newcome's mind. There is a far-off echo of that inevitable San Sisto face in the sister Raphael Madonna, the foligno in the Vatican of Rome. But it is not the same, for nothing can be. Poor Heine, even! How want of faith—I don't mean in religion only—is apt to break down at its best! When he describes the Virgin-mother—mystery or fraud—as the "dame du comptoir" of the Raphaeline painters, decked up in prettiness to attract the custom, it becomes difficult—to me—to imagine a poet's humour gone more prosaically wrong. I could sing, Homerically enough, and by the hour together, of all the other treasures of the Dresden temple, of Rubens's rich Gardens of Armida, of the two lovely Mag-dalens of Correggio and Battoni, giving the unwilling palm, perhaps, to the least famous, of the melting Potiphar's young wife of Carlo Cignani, probably the only presentment of that forbidding and forbidden tale which makes us speculate why Joseph was such a fool as to run away; but the Sistine Madonna reigns with me imperious and supreme, as she did when first I met her full forty years ago. And so completely has she fascinated my remembrance, and led me through other bird's-eye views of other arts into discursions quite beside the mark, that I must defer my Prison experience for another chapter.

CHAPTER XV

DISSOLVING VIEWS

IT was on a pleasant evening in the leafy month of July that two cavaliers of similar ages, though mayhap the one may have had the advantage of some two years over his companion, might have been seen strolling with leisurely footsteps across the Bridge of Dresden. The taller of the two was classically handsome, with a slight moustache of down shading the curved upper lip, and deerlike eyes that seemed to be looking into futurity. I wis not that they were truly absorbed in any such abstruse contemplation, but rather in inward thought about the beauties of his own person. Crisp curling hair, a dark shade of brown, clung to his temples and his small but shapely head under its covering of Sombrero form. His companion laid no claim to these physical advantages, though roundness and confidence were transparent in every curve of his less perfectly moulded form. At which point unfortunately the strings of my lute must change to what happened to me since I wrote down those two last words.

Two years ago, as I have said, I lost every farthing by frauds which I was left to follow out for myself, if possible. At last, after two years of Hope and Work, I arrived at a Court of—Justice, and asked for a bond back of just five hundred pounds, traced beyond question to a gentleman who disposed of my goods, knowing exactly whose they were; being, indeed, himself a friend of the defaulter. That defaulter walks abroad a free unhampered man, having been first whitewashed by the Society of Law.

The one bond of five hundred pounds of what had been appropriated, it was thought on all hands I must recover, as it was traced, and its real ownership not denied; but on some legal plea I was refused all restitution and fined heavily in "costs" for asking for it!

That trouble broke me finally and entirely. The lawyers have now restored me four pounds, out of their own takings of some twenty thousand, to appeal with! The humour of the dogs! Some of them are sorry, but pass by upon the other side.

Thackeray must have been hovering about me when I started on this chapter, in the very spirit of his Papa Fielding, for in one of Dicky Doyle's delightful little initial sketches do I find good Colonel Newcome and the bonny Clive riding home together in just such romantic guise, side by side, upon old Thomas's return from India, by way of Malta, with his boy, whereanent, by-the-bye, I am sorry to find our Clive—somewhere about this time—proclaiming Titian's " Assumption " as the finest picture in the world. He was not as true to Raphael as to Ethel, after all So did that youthful pair of Oxford undergraduates stroll across the Dresden bridge in innocence, bent on a pipe and Lager in the beer gardens of the riverside. Two-thirds across, and in the gloaming, they were accosted by two minions in helmets, of the Saxon law, who, with strange gestures, sent us to the other side of the bridge, as being on the wrong one. Not understanding, we crossed as bidden, and turned back again. Then they descended on us again for being always on the wrong side, out of contumacy, and when I remonstrated in doubtful but rather wrathful German, swore that I knocked them down, and took me up. I spent the night in prison with a truckle-bed, a jug of water, a loaf of black bread, a German Bible, and a list of warnings to prisoners, telling me that I should be punished with various degrees of corporal punishment if I objected I was released after some fifteen hours of durance, spent chiefly, as I think, in throwing black pellets of bread out between the bars at puzzled old vendresses in the market-place below. My friend got me the help of an alarmed Saxon friend, and I was released after severe examination through an interpreter, in which I was called upon to swear, amongst other things, that there was no such rule on London Bridge as having to walk on different sides each way ; that every Londoner didn't take his constitutional over London Bridge and back every day was what the examiner simply refused to believe. Obviously I was too deceitful. The English Minister told me afterwards that if I cared to stay in Dresden it would be a casus belli. My case filled many German folios. I fear I didn't care, and left the land. Another question I was asked, as through interpreter, was if I had " ever been transported." " Not to my knowledge " was all that I could say. What the

Herr meant was, " Had I ever been in prison ?" "No, I had not thus far "; though it might mean worse than that. It is the only thing, as far as I can see, that die Fates had left themselves to do with me. What for, except for having been pillaged all round, I know not yet, nor ever shall now. But we live in tyrannous times, all said and done.

Another of my long vacations was spent among the echoes of Killarney, in company of Lyulph Stanley, since of School Board fame. Pleasantly entertained at Muckross, the Herberts' seat, we climbed Tore and Mac Gillicuddy, boated on the Lakes, tracked out the scenes of The Collegians, or assisted at the regattas of Ken-mare. Comfortably thriving on Scholarship derived from Vaughaa and confirmed by Merry, I had attained then to a first class in the classic school of Moderations, and had rather prematurely made up my mind that the rest of my college course would be, as old folk said, in a concatenation accordingly. Stanley, on the contrary, had but emerged a second, and set to work at once to remedy the error. Whence it was that, dreaming still, I found myself at the second scholastic crisis relegated only to the second grade of the Humaner Letters, while he secured his first What difference it makes much afterwards, even in a whirling world, I know not. In chat Killarney year I took one term of grace, and in the later summer, in the kind charge of a dear old cousin, Baron Heath, once Governor of the Bank of England, for many years Italian Consul in London, and a model of the old-world courtesies, was carried off in guise of secretary, after a brief descent on Berne, to Spain. There was a brief interval of a visit to the Stanleys' place at Alderley, remembered by me chiefly for a meeting with the famous Mrs. Grote. Celebrities of all kinds met in the Stanley house. That strong-mind-edest of ladies, great in her way as *ha*historian husband, was to arrive for dinner. She was late, and when she came, came in a sort of Alpine guise. The explanation to her hostess was that she had intended to walk from the station, with her chattels to follow, but, finding herself tired and muddy, had accepted a lift in a carrier's cart that was passing. She was not perturbed, and questioned me about the company. Among them was an R.A. rising into fame, who had been some three weeks in the house, engaged upon a sylvan study in the woods of Alderley. " What," said Mrs. Grote to me in her deep bass voice, "three weeks staying here to paint one treel Mr. Painter knows when he's well oft"

I have every reason to believe that my Consul Cousin could have done very well without a secretary. It was one of those acts of gracious kindness, of which I have met with many in the world, to counteract wrong and evil, where one expects it least Therefore one must make the best or worst of it, and let the results alone.

In my capacity of secretary I only remember writing one letter for my baronial cousin in our four months of wandering by grace. Restless always, I suppose that I overdid everything, to make it needful. The letter was from Madrid, and written to Michael Costa, the famous orchestral auto-crat of Gye the elder's Covent Garden. My cousin was a fine musician, a great Maecenas of the art All the best singers and virtuists of the day congregated at his big double house in Russell Square, where there were palaces of magnates then. I remember me of one brilliant amateur, re-joicing in the full-mouthed Italian name of the Countess Amalia Brancaleoni, who was broken-hearted because, unlike the as son-orous and as noble Marietta Piccolomini, she could not escape from the wind of her nobility and go upon the stage. What advantage these foreign damsels do possess over us in way of names! What could it be to a man, for instance, to love a Julia Thompson after losing his heart to an Adelgunda Marwede and Antoinetta Constantino ? La Brancaleoni had a voice, note for note, the same as that of her historic contemporary, the great contralto Alboni. And her delight was to stand in the middle of the room while one of my cousins accompanied her, and—acting and singing both—to pour out in golden volume her impassioned gift of song. The brindisi from Lucrezia Borgia— the haunting "Che faro" of Gläck, the Arsace strains from Semiramide—she would give me them one after another, while I sate young and open-mouthed in a corner, just devouring, like J. J. Ridley in Thackeray's story.

It was about another singer—and music, of one sort or another, seems an especial ornament of Christmas-tide—that I wrote from Madrid the solitary epistle which earned me my first Spanish tour for nothing on a scale of regal magnificence. For my cousin was one of the old commercial princes, and carried his courier with him as well as his secretary wherever we went. The courier did everything the secretary didn't, and the latter official had a high old time. There wasn't much to eat and drink in Spain in those days, but what there was he got So at Madrid we went to the Italian opera. There were Italian operas everywhere then. And we heard Grisi and Mario in the Huguenots—not for the first time, I admit; but the treat was not one that staled Baron Heath was curious about the page Urbano, of whom we had heard as a promising and clever French girl. And when a long-legged and gawky but pretty dark-eyed miss of some sixteen came on to treat us to her opening song, in a voice as rich and fresh as a young organ, his practised taste detected such high promise through the youthfulness of Mlle. Trivelle, that he made me write that letter to the imperious conductor, and tell him to send to Madrid and look out for Alboni's successor. And Costa's answer was to laugh at his friend's enthusiasm for way-side genius. But within a very few seasons the pretty maypole made her appearance at the rival house—Her Majesty's—under the banners of Mapleson, and as the Italianised Trebelli. Costa admitted to feeling very sore.

The cosas d'España, *or things of Spain, were in a queer state then. The few railways there were began and ended in the most unlikely places, for no particular reason. One costly iron road ran about fifteen minutes out of Barcelona, and then stopped. You lumbered along vile roads in topheavy diligences, with your driver sitting behind his horsed with a bagful of sharp stones, which he aimed at the sore places on the poor brutes' backs to make them go on ; or you coasted from Barcelona to Valencia in a ghastly little steamer, which meant sea-sickness in every creak and swell, all the principal ships being taken for transports, as a war was coming off in Morocco. The people hated it, and were not even stirred by the dithyrambs of the papers, which fanned their ardour by descriptions of the Moorish maidens, with* " ojos neros y passiones vehe-mentes" eagerly and with open arms awaiting the Spanish conqueror. The Spanish conqueror didn't want to go, and didn't care whether the arms of the maidens opened or not; but he submitted in his fatalistic way, and my cousin and I saw a mighty function in the public place of Valentia, with the Cardinal-Archbishop blessing the standards, and a big disembarkation from the port of the Grao afterwards. It was a varied feast of colour.

It was a pleasant introduction to a country centuries behind everybody else, though the hardier North asserted itself even then, and Barcelona was well ahead of what Malaga is now. Only the other day a Spanish barber here in London objected altogether to my calling him a Spaniard He was from Barcelona, and a Catalan. And if the lazy Southerners, and the miserable jobbers of Madrid, would only allow of the election of a pure Catalan Government, they would soon then see, quoth he, what the old Empress of the Earth could do. Well, there seems to be a Spanish revival coming. Business is lord just now ; and after English, the Spanish, increasing in circulation every day, is the language most in demand with business men. And Perea Nena the peerless danced for us in Barcelona, and Neri Baraldi sang; and the Consul at the foot of Montserrat gave us a pleasant welcome for the night before our climb. And his pretty blonde daughter, known in the neighbourhood as the White Angel for colouring so unusual there, clearly held me guilty of high treason for falling in love for the evening, and all the next day, with a seductive dark-eyed cousin used to the second fiddle, and delighted to play the first for once. She was newer to my Anglo Saxon taste. Her *ojos* were *neros* to the point of distraction. Whether her *passianes* were *vehemcntes* I had not time to arrive at the point of asking. But she was very nice, and taught-me all the Spanish I knew for many years.

We did not reach the southern provinces, for from Valencia our business programme carried us to Madrid, allowing us before we left to sample Murviedro, the old seaside Saguntum so long abandoned by the sea. There we had to put up in an amazing old shanty suggestive of the last act of Rigoletto,- two rooms one over the other with no fourth side. The family and the horses slept in the lower room, the Baron and I and the courier and the pigs in the upper. I wonder if there is a hotel there now. Spain's only railway took us to Madrid, and there, divided between the historic desolations of Toledo and the Escorial, and the insatiable delights of the picture gallery and the seductions of the Italian opera and the native dancers and, I am ashamed to say, of the unholy bull-ring, I had, for a busy secretary, a very pleasant time.

As Fate would have it, the subject for the next year's Oxford Newdigate was the Escorial My friends all thought that I was bound to get it, though at that time I had not embarked upon the sea of poetry. However, I wrote four lines, and thus:

I was alone; scarce on my ear had died
The untaught accents of my chattering guide,
Who held discourse of emperors and kings
As unrespected and familiar things.

At that point I consulted an expert, who said that familiarity of that kind was all very well for Goldsmith, but would never do for Newdigate. So I went no farther, and did not even send my quatrain in.

But I remember that, when the successful Newdigate of my year was recited, I thought but little of it. It did not remind me of the real Escorial at all, but soared on the wings of the most unchartered British imagination. It would have applied equally to Hampton Court, but it was truly classical and ten-syllabled, and was the work of a good man and true, John Addington Symonds.

We left Madrid by diligence. We left it at half-past nine on a Wednesday morning, and reached Bayonne at half-past four on Saturday afternoon. It was a good deal of carriage exercise for one bout But with the whole of a cold coupé to ourselves, stoppages at Burgos and a few other places, and en-livened by a mighty forest fire by night as we crossed the Pyrenees, we got through the long, monotonous, sandy desert of a track by constant recourse to cold chicken and red wine. But oh, how my bones ached! Oh, how tired I was! Oh, how unutterably grim and dirty! We have all read much of soldiers' marches of late, but it would take many marches over many lands to beat seventy-nine hours of a Spanish diligence some forty years ago. After all those weeks of Spanish fare, our dinner at Bayonne that Saturday night has passed with me into a religious memory. And my cousin the Consul and Baron knew, amongst other things, how to order, and to eat, a dinner. Christmas Day was upon us when I parted with my dear and generous old host in the good city of Bayonne, after a peep at unfledged Biarritz-on-Sea, and made my way across the South of France to Nice. Railway communication ended just beyond Marseilles, and again the ancient diligence rattled and rumbled me along—along by the sparkling Mediterranean, and under the green Estrelles, through lovely and unfashionable

Cannes—where nobody lived then except a few fishermen and Lord Brougham—letting you savour the beauties of the scenery after a method quite forgotten now. And when we crossed the river Var on the unsafe old bridge, which was but a weak barrier between two fair kingdoms then, I was for the first time in my life in Italy, within a few weeks to be Italy no more. How changed it is, all that! The Promenade des Anglais was a rough, half-finished road. My mother —an invalid, whom I had gone to join—had a large first floor in the Maison Laurençin, the corner house of the Promenade and the Quai Masséia, which is now one of the biggest of the Nice hotels. Bridge over the Paglione's mouth there was none. Only the predecessor of that a little way above, close to the Hotel Chauvain, then monarch of all that it surveyed in the hotel way. Is not its name changed now ? I fancy so. Carabaçel was lanes and scattered houses. The only Villafranca road wound over the dividing hills. Nor road nor rail led on to Monaco or to Mentone, and Monte Carlo was an uninvented word. The beautiful Cornice was the only way. And you dropped upon Monaco on foot, scrambling down the hills Turbii. As one looked upon the little nestling water-gem, one wanted to take a header into it.

National little Nice was considerably ex-cited then. She hated to be transferred in the cause of Italian unity, and was bitter enough about a union that meant for her divorce. Cavour's great stroke of policy was a bad pill to her, and savage Nationalists were to be met in many drawing-rooms. Suzanni, brother tribune of Saffi and Mazzini, interested me much, though, naturally, he was reserved with me. Garibaldi himself, greatest of all Nisards—of all men in the world, therefore, hating that annexation most, seeming as it did ingratitude indeed to him—was in the town when first I came, and I watched him playing bowls with his chums in his shirt-sleeves—"quite like a common chap," as one of my companions said And there were times during that winter when the ferment became dangerous. Some of the larger tradesmen took secret pleasure in the change, but scarcely cared to say so. But the game had been well played, and the guards well drilled, and the precautions were well taken. And when the French troops marched into the town, it was with all the show of bunting and of flags common to all festive occasions. But the faces! It was pain to watch them. Sad, sullen, dejected, wild. It was a triumphal entry into a conquered town. And the iron plough of the conqueror went over Nisza Mar.

But fashionable Nice, save for far smaller proportions of Mob, was what it is, and was, and will be. Only the outside trappings of Dame Fashion change. She is but a dainty skirt-dancer before the throne of Policies. The first thing that happened to me was to have a dancing-master sent for, to show me how to waltz. Fresh from the tennis-courts and cricket-fields, I had small turn that way. But there was to be a dance in our own rooms next day—the feminine pressure was put on—and in a very shamefaced fashion I went through the drill. And, in my usual go-ahead way, I took a sudden fancy to the waltz, and for the next three months seemed to be doing nothing else every night, except when it was La Boccabadati in the *Traviata* or Levassor in his French vaudevilles. And when the season closed, so rapid had been my development that I found myself not only dancing in the rainbow cotillons, but leading them, a premiership which was often to be my lot afterwards in the less picturesque surroundings of London. And during those halcyon days there were picnics on the hills or saunters in the castle, and boats to Villafranca, and donkey-rides (donkey-rides at Nice!) into the fair interior, day after day, and everything that seemed least like Christmas to one who had never Christmased it out of England before. Of all my sweet girl-partners, of course I liked one the best, and we loved each other all the season through. I wrote small and early verse about her, and, as I learnt by surreptitious means, she talked about me to her maid when she was in her morning bath. She was very young and very pretty, and the houri of Montserrat faded from my inconstant mind. I need not say that nothing came of it but vows, which at that age don't count When some years afterwards we met again, it was to laugh.

> For in my heart's remotest cell
> There had been many different lodgers,
> And she was not the drawing-room belle,
> But only Mrs. Something Rogers.

Music, of course, was a great fact at Nice. Sofie Cruvelli—by her true German name Cräwel—led the van, and, as the Baroness Vigier, was the great lady who gave concerts. A few years before she had convulsed all Lumley-London and the omnibus-boxers by running away and disappearing in the middle of the season. Impresarios went wild and epigrammatists made jokes, and " Where's Cruvelli ?" was the skit of the day. She got married, and gave up the show. But twice in the year she gave a public concert at Nice and sang her old songs. She was a fine, full woman, with blue-black hair and eyes, and one of those effortless voices which come out of themselves. Like the two daughters of Garcia, Malibran and Viardot, she had the double register. Alboni tried for it, but failed, and her *Somnambula* broke down,' as well as nearly breaking down Amina's bridge through her specific gravity. But Cruvelli, like the Garcias, would sing Semiramide or Arsace indifferently. The theatre *prima donna,* La Boccabadati, was quite a great actress with a small sweet voice, adored by the Niçois gods, while the young baritone, Cotogni, afterwards made himself a London name. The tenor was like most tenors, fat and awful.

Italian names certainly sound better than English. Boccabadati is more distinguished than Take-care-of-your-mouth, even as Tag-liafico, that most ail-roundly useful of all basses, who sang and acted everything in turn, and ended as a stage-manager, had a more convincing way with him than Cut-fig. But my musical heroine of Nice was an Englishwoman, Clara Novello. Even to this day she is, of all the minstrels, my most abiding memory. Of later singers, the voice of Titiens resembled hers the most in its full power of penetrating sound. She filled the Crystal Palace, as Clara Novello could fill anything when she was empress of Exeter Hall. But the art of Titiens was very imperfect indeed, while the others was perfection. Curious to think that the last of the greatest oratorio-quartette (taking the four together) ever heard has but lately disappeared from us : Clara Novello; Miss Dolby; Herr Formes; and Sims Reeves. The retired English singer—Countess Gigliucci, by her married style—was very kind to me at Nice; and used to give me tea at what she called her little button of a house among the hills. And then she would sit at the piano, and sing me ballad after ballad of the simpler kind, in a voice which she could modulate for a Pyramid or a nutshell, till the pleasure of music became almost a pain. No wonder, after my young advantages, that I am sometimes difficult to please.

Just at the end of my stay, two chums and I tramped the Cornice road as far as San Remo, as it existed then. Returning, we stayed at Monaco. Monte Carlo was a rock, barren apd anonymous. Monaco was a, tiny, if independent, empire, with a few houses, a prince, a standing army of some six, and a seedy roulette-room. We played there daringly. There was nobody else there, except two or three seedier croupiers, who obviously lost on purpose, to draw us on. We were drawn on till we had recouped ourselves in the full expenses of our little walking tour. Then we pocketed our gains, buttoned our breeches, and withdrew, as both joyfuller and wiser men. The croupiers looked seedier and sadder as we went And(a panting little Mediterranean steamboat carried me from newly-Frenchified Nice harbour to Marseilles, and I went back to England to resume my Oxford life, with a mind rather singularly opened by a little circle of winter travel, unusual for an undergraduate of that less gaddish day.

CHAPTER XVI

MATTHEW ARNOLD AND THE NORFOLK CIRCUIT

LET me proceed with my chronicle while time is left. My scholar times at Oxford, such as they may have been, were spent, as has been my way of life, with older men. Youth had its fling in odd forms, as things went. We were much impressed by a sermon of the famous Mr. Spurgeon, in which he said there would be no harm in dancing if the sexes mixed not, but only danced apart. We took that hint, and did; inaugurating Spurgeon balls in Balliol. Lyrist and dramatist afterwards, Robert Reece would take the piano. The youths who stood for ladies took their coats off for a sign, and we danced into the small hours merrily enough. Bouncers and Jokers were ever to the fore. Then, the theatricals! Unknown before, we brought them into Balliol under the tutelary care of a strolling actor who came to Oxford • with an entertainment and stage-managed us. He was short and red and earnest, and said that within a few years he would be dead or famous. I never heard of him again, so I suppose he's dead. We enacted an Olympic playlet of Tom Taylor's, called *To Oblige Benson,* and a farce of the day called *Crinoline.* Our cast included, amongst others, two who became playwrights, one who turned solicitor, an Egyptian judge, a man of fashion, a distinguished Civil servant, and a headmaster. The latter was our *jeune premier,* a strong-knit and determined man, great in the 'Varsity eight as on all rivers afterwards, who practically bossed the undergraduate forces of the college from a fixed purpose to have his own way in everything. I do not know that he was a great scholar; but when he told the examiners to give him a first class, they did. He certainly was not a great actor; but we engaged him out of policy, otherwise we might not have been allowed to act. Still in my mind's eye I can see his stalwart figure now, in a frock-coat and a violent perspiration, stammering out something inaudibly *his jeune premier's* creed: "Where women are concerned, I am inflammable. And glory in it." And he is head-master at Eton now.

The little red professional made us all up. And Toody, as in To Oblige Benson my fair wife was called, looked, in a wig of close curls, I must say more wildly unfeminine than any performer I remember. We got some regular scenery down from London. The larger gates of the college, which was much excited, had to be opened to let that scenery in. That more distressed our dear mild college Dean than anything connected with the show. "Tay tay!" he said, with a strange interjection that belonged to him, "those gates have only been opened once before in my memory, when the Prince Consort came!" It was an odd performance, I should think, though we had crowded houses for two nights under difficulties, since illness took us from the staircase chosen only the day before. And in the space of time remaining to us, our theatre had to be moved bodily to other rooms hard by, and cut about to suit the new proportions.

Sad, possibly, was the result of that brief theatric frenzy, the seed of the Drama in classic and ecclesiastic Oxford. We were more stern than Cambridge, which about that time, under Burnandian and kindred auspices, started upon its famous A.D.C. We wanted one, but Dame Oxford, more pedant or more prudent than Dame Cambridge, said us nay. So some of us indulged our proclivities by forming a little club of our own, and acting in other towns when we could get the chance. I have no reason to think that our performances were great. The strangest was the last I had just taken my degree as Bachelor of Arts, when, with Reece and Ponsonby and another,

I joined a provincial company for the fun of it, touring at Leamington and Coventry under our red friend's management. Leamington was distinctly fashionable ; Coventry was distinctly not. At the first city all was as it should be ; at the second it was nothing of the kind. At Leamington our houses were full; at Coventry they were exceeding empty. Touring companies, be it remembered, were not the functions that they now are. They were still the days of the Bingleys and the Snevellicci

We added a new farce to our Coventry repertory, and as Reece, who had not been with us at Leamington, was to bring the only book with him from town for study the night before, much depended on him. He did not arrive until the day of the performance at midday. We rushed upon the book to copy out our parts, and then and there discovered that there was one more woman in the play than there was in the company. A brief and summary consultation resulted in our dressing up our red-polled manager in female guise, and in the evening on we went, our parts concealed on scrip beneath our hats, unconscious of all save cues. I remember suddenly coming across in mine a passage which made necessary a glass of sherry at the wing. A local swell was lounging at that entrance, and I rushed up to him. " Have you," I said, " anything about you like a glass of sherry ? " The audience roared. "Well, no," he answered ; "would a cigar do as well? " " It would," I said, and took one, which I lit. So we got through that drama. Ponsonby, who had no part in that especial play, was seated in the dress circle next an old gentleman in wrath. " Oxford amateurs," said he; " why, it's disgraceful! They don't know one syllable of all their parts between them." Pon-sonby turned round to him and shook hands. "You are quite right, sir," said he; "that is the most sensible remark I've heard since I have been in Coventry." Oh, those days!

Finding a tail-coat wanted in one piece, Ponsonby borrowed a frock-coat from our landlord and stuck the back halves up with pins. At another crisis, in a costume piece in two acts, called, as I think, **Our Wife,** clever but not consecutive, we got so mixed at one point in Act One, that those of us who were on the stage stuck fast. Ponsonby brought on all the company at once. And we finished the first Act with a brilliant finale, which properly belonged to the second. The applause on fall of curtain was all that could be desired. And when the situation recurred in Act the

Second, we did that scene again. Nobody found it out!

Still we were not a success at Coventry. The weavers didn't like us, and gathered round our lattice at the inn at night, even so far as throwing stones at us. We bore it bravely, and for the next night sent out double orders without result Nobody used them. So, as the fair was on, we walked through it two and two, beating drums and blowing trumpets. And yet they came not. We picknicked, all of us, at Kenilworth, and the leading lady played Juliet to my Romeo from a ruined window, to the amazement of some honest families about. We wound up our engagement with a dance upon the stage, the band from Leamington having come over in our honour. We danced into the night, and I yet.remember our boldest in his shirt-sleeves, a tankard of beer beside him, waltzing with the critic of the ***Coventry Herald!***

The company had to be left behind at Coventry in pawn, and when we four got back to Leamington, we bailed it out. On our return to Oxford as we should be, we raised a dummy in the corner-seat of the train. We set up a great-coat in sitting attitude, and covered our leading lady's muff on the top of it, looking just like back hair, with a tall hat leaning down over it. We inflated a glove, and set a cigar between the fingers and a ticket in the hatband. And then we threw a rug across the figure. When the guard asked for tickets, we said the man was ill, and we dared not disturb him. The guard declared that he must, and crossed between us. Then roused the dummy, who fell into bits. From Oxford, afterwards, I had to take the train and travel across country, to join a circuit of another kind—the NorfolkCircuitat Norwich, as judge's marshal to Chief Justice Erle, justest and kindliest of magnates both, there to make my first acquaintance with Matthew Arnold as my brother-marshal. And the strange hunt in quest of scholarships, and the friends many and various, and the racquets and the fields and walks, and the tennis with Tomkins and with Barre, ended with the days of Oxford. Magdalen walks and Christ-church meadows! blending streams of Cherwell and of Isis, with all the mellow mystery of bells, wonderful gardens of Trinity under the academic eaves, you were a dream, too much of one, before utility! As it so happened, I saw but little of Oxford afterwards—rrmore of the sister University, and the prevalence of trams and bicycles, and of the fair sex, has changed things in the oddest way. The ladies are everywhere now. As far as I remember, there was about six who counted, in my day ; three of them very pretty.

Chief Justice Erie's was a great figure in my youth. Rough and of country accent, always for justice before letter-law when he could pierce to it Sprung of the Western Circuit, almost as great a nurse of legal eminence in those days as Balliol of classic, he was of heart and conscience singularly tender. His fellow-judge upon the Norfolk Circuit was Judge Wightman, an old man then, and father-in-law of Matthew Arnold, who accompanied him on circuit as marshal, famous as he was in other ways. Every evening, after the day's work was over, we four—four different generations of life—sate down to our rubbers in the judges' lodgings. My whist was very primitive, I fear, but good enough for a fourth hand in such good company. My chiefs first recourse, when his cards were dealt to him, was to groan audibly, and as he played them out—an ace at a time, perhaps, for luck was often with him—to groan more sadly over every trick he wo. When he did not win he was given to the use of Anglo-Saxon of a sturdy kind indeed, at which good old Judge Wight-man would hold up his hands with a remonstrance, " Oh brother, brother." And Arnold smiled his pleasant smile of watchful humour, and I wondered to myself how such a small and early f3ish out of the water as I had somehow swum into such goodly company. It was Erie's wont to take two horses with him on his circuits, one for himself and another for his marshal, and ride from town to town, besides taking his own daily ride before the sittings of the court. The last duty he proceeded at once to let me off unless I should be so disposed, as he did even that of abstracting the pleadings, which was the marshal's one title, I believe, to his professional earnings at the time. He was infinitely kind and considerate to the youngster as to everybody, and frankly told me that he didn't think my abstracts assisted justice in the least Any miscarriage of justice, any failure of his own to convince a jury on a point which he felt just and right, haunted him like a personal pain. He would talk of it, even to me, for days. His may have been an exceptional figure in that way at any time perhaps; certainly one does not look upon his like again just now.

Our rides from town to town were curious feats. Erie steadily proceeded at a swing trot always, on beasts of stolid mould accustomed to it He stuck his elbows bravely out and groaned at intervals, as over whist. One day, riding from Cambridge as I think it was, a youthful desire seized on me to get on faster just for once. A convenient stretch of turf for cantering bordered the road just there, and, without wavering, I put my wondering beast into the swing. He was sur-prised, no doubt, but not displeased. He had a little tired of the old pace too. But as we bowled along we heard the voice of the good judge behind us. We turned deaf ears and would not wind up till our quickened canter had well finished. I expected severe reproaches from my companion, whose kindness for animals was like the rest of him. He only muttered a good deal on the subject, that I had taught him a lesson. His horses had been taking him in. They could canter or gallop as well as any other man's, but had malingered till he quite thought they couldn't On one of our rides we crossed a ferry, and for some reason the judge deposited a small coin on the ferryman's window-sill. I remember thinking it was unlike his usual liberality, and we rode on in silence for a little way. Then he suddenly stopped, " Did I give that poor fellow enough ? " he said to me. And as I suppose my answer was doubtful, we had to ride back again to let him increase his *largesse*.

The pleasant companionship of Matthew Arnold lightened that circuit even for so young a man. I am not sure of the judgment that stamps him among the greatest of the poets by the side of so great a one as Tennyson, but with all his many and prosaic avocations he had not the time and leisure to cultivate the Muse as exclusively as nearly all of her prime favourites have done; all I think really, for I can recall for the moment none but Milton perhaps, who did much of hard work in other fields, And Milton's politics did his verse no good. Arnold's was a very attractive figure to those who knew him well From the time of that early circuit I grew to be close friends with himself and his family, and saw much of them in London, and at the Arnold home in Lakeland at Fox-How by Rydal. There do I much remember that we all ensued croquet, then in its vigorous infancy, under conditions which would not be favourable to its more scientific sides, for we played chiefly in umbrellas and very thick boots, on the slope of a hill declining on the lake. The effect of what we then called a tight-croquet down the mountain side was in its way unique, waking the echoes of those fir surroundings to a music of its own, one of the little boy Arnolds, " Let me tooky loo! let me tooky loo !"—" Croquet you " being intended, often coming back upon my ear. Matthew Arnold's was the most evenly cheerful disposition I have ever known, never in high spirits as I remember him, and never in low ; with a vein of grave and scholarly humanity always in his talk, with his children showing itself in the form of a caressing companionship, and with his affect tionate and gentle wife in the tenderest and most equable of intimacies. Theirs was the ideal of a quiet and trustful home, I think, and a lesson in harmony to the less fortunate. It was for his boys—one of them, a young musical genius, suffered from chronic heart-disease of which at last he died, still in his boyhood, and was therefore the rrjost watched one of the flock—that he wrote his perfect quatrain about the "felis tigris" of the household.

> Cruel, but composed and bland,
> Calm, unspeakable, and grand,
> So Tiberius might have sate,
> Had Tiberius been a cat.

With all his own work to do, Arnold was not much visible on circuit, except at the evening whist, to me—though I saw enough of him to lay the foundations of the alliance. Occasionally, as representatives of the judicial arm, we were bidden to the feasts and boards of the nobility and gentry of Debrett, either with the dignitaries or without them, as once to the Rothschild gem of a *villeg-gtatura* at Aston Clinton, changed, no doubt, though how I know not, since that day, with its gems of painting and statuary, and its bath of inlaid marble built over a natural spring of purest water, a curiosity of luxury, as I remember thinking, worthy of ancient Rome. Arnold was an amusing talker on the subject of the Drama, caring admittedly only for the classic He looked upon the *cothurnus* as the truest analyst of the perplexities and destinies of life, and had small sympathy, which was odd in him, with the laughing portraits of the Muse of Comedy, which had: in them to him something of the nature of mere caricature at best The plays of Aristophanes were in reality but satire in burlesque, and even the comedies of Moliére were to him but as weaker imitations. Twice only in my memory of him do I remember his going to the theatre; once, because our alliance induced him to ask me for a box to see a modern-life play of mine and Craufurd Grove's then strongly running at one of the London theatres. He expressed himself afterwards to have been very much entertained, and interested too, but placidly observed that he had been most struck by the improbabilities, that is the unfailing companions of the Drama, which to my old ex-perience seem more in attendance nowadays than ever. But people forget that a play is an epitome of a mere corner of time enlarged but in imagination, and that to touch the probable at all is as much as can be expected of it " People don't do such things " is the quieter comment on half the plays of nowadays. The nearest thing to do is not to be impossible. How can you be real in a room with only three sides to it ? Well, 1 fell into my error in good company in that case. Baron Martin, the famous Yorkshire racing judge, had before him a case in which counsel quoted *Romeo and Juliet.* He said that he had heard of it but never read it; and as the case was adjourned on the rising of the court, would do so that night, and tell them what he thought about it the next morning. Whereon he opened the proceedings by remarking in his broad Yorkshire: " I've read your *Romeo and Juliet,* and don't think much of ut. It's a tissue of improbabilities from the beginning to the end." A revivable old anecdote at this distance of the time. From his own more refined and scholarly points of view, Matthew Arnold could be guilty of heresies in the great Shakespeare cult almost as daring, for his other visit to the play that I remember brought one out I saw him one day on the opposite side of the street, pacing along and smiling to himself in the way I knew so well. Amused I went across to him and asked him what had happened "What is the fun?" I said. " Have they been attacking you again in the Saturday ?" For to break lances with that periodical was an amusement to both; Freeman, the historian, being reputed to be his adversary. " Oh no, my dear boy, no! 1 went to Drury Lane last night" " Oh I to see Helen Faucit in *Cymbeline ?* Didn't you admire her?" "Oh, not that—poor dear lady "—in his inimitable *longueurs,* which could not be described as a drawl—" she was charming, of course. But it's the play, you know, Cymbeline / Such an odd, broken-backed sort of a thing! It couldn't have happened anywhere, you know." And, indeed, such a stricture is not unjustified by the too wholesale admirers even of Shakespeare himself. A little book might be added to the already burdened list, called "The Dull Plays of Shakespeare." Amongst even those, however, *Cymbeline* has one distinction. If *Hamlet was* said by the neophyte as being " so full of quotations," *Cymbeline,* with the exception of Fidele's dirge, does not, as far as I know, contain a single remembered touch, which makes me doubt the Master's presence altogether. *The Winter's Tale,* for instance, which must, I think, on the whole be admitted to be an inferior play too, teems with such gems and extracts all the way through. But Shakespeare's claim to undisputed primacy rests on his best. Four masterpieces of tragedy, each with its keynote : the tragedy of love, *Romeo and Juliet;* of madness, *Lear* ; of jealousy, *Othello ;* and of destiny, *Hamlet*. In comedy, *As You Like It, Much Ado, and Twelfth Night,* we have three. Historical chronicle in dramatic shape attains its highest in *Richard the Third.* And the realms of fancy never supplied two such dreams of the poet's imagination as *The Tempest* and the *Midsummer Night.* That variety of Shakespeare's mind was of all its greatest marvel. To have struck on such a fairy-mine as the last of these would have been to any other writer a career for life. It was enough for him to strike it, and to pass. But then such masterpieces from one hand are enough for the very greatest fame. Neither a Shakespeare nor a Michael Angelo can always attain to that

CHAPTER XVII

WANDERING MEMORIES

THE chambers of the usual conveyancer in Lincoln's Inn, and the usual pleader in the ." Temple," with the help of the course of dinners prescribed for the full honours of barristership, followed upon my departure from Oxford. My conveyancer was a famous character in his way, a bachelor devoted to his friends and his hospitalities, living himself in his modest lodgings, and alternating between them and chambers, delighting in large hospitalities to big parties of young men and maidens, well and truly chosen, for the theatre or the Crystal Palace, the grounds of which, under his genial auspices, were the scene of many a cheery feast and many a pleasant flirtation. Kettle ended sadly by losing his fortunes through the usual treacherous friend for whom he went security, and passed quietly away one evening suddenly, with a smile upon his face, to leave a host of regretful friends behind him. He prided himself, in spite of the nature of his gatherings, on forming a school of young bachelors who were to forswear marriage and follow his example, and eschew the fair sex for a pleasant friendship or a bright companionship. His scholars were all ardent in their vows of fidelity to the precept, but out of some half-dozen only one has kept them. Precept, I fear, was scarcely strong enough for temptation; and the long summer evenings in the Crystal Palace grounds, smiling on young couples wandering apart in twilight, after a Lucullus feast within glass, prolonged delightfully up to the latest train, were not devised to breed a taste for solitary life. Kettle himself was the typical old bachelor of the hospitable type, and so universal a favourite with women that he might well be excused for an insufficient devotion to any one of them. In his chambers he was a hard and rapid worker, with a power of concentration; once in his papers, he seemed neither to hear nor see anything that passed in his room, or notice the presence of anybody, which helped him to do the work of three men in the time of one. Otherwise a dry and observant humorist, as true a Londoner as Major Pendennis himself, never to be taken off his guard. Once he was asked on a matter of business to stay at the country house of an engineer in the North, and when he had made himself very agreeable at dinner, and the company were retiring, the ladies to their bedroom gossips and the men to the smoking-room, his hostess said to him over the good-night, " Mr.. Kettle, we always breakfast at eight o'clock." " Do you, dear lady!" he answered with a Chesterfield salute; " I never do." And at the same visit he wad credited with an heretical opinion about the usual after-dinner pianoforte work, more general, perhaps, than natural gifts allow. When the usual young-lady melodies began, he retired into the remotest corner he could find, and with a newspaper. " I'm afraid, Mr. Kettle, you don't care about music?" "Indeed I do, madam," he said with polite warmth, " I can't bear it" Musical articulation certainly justifies the cynic in a way, in spite of Shakespeare's condemnation. " Vewy chawming," as the kid-gloved exquisite said to the pretty drawing-room singer after she had indulged the company with Kingsley's "Three Fishers." But what silly choruses there are now I What does she mean by "Hah-bah-bah?"

We were primitive pupils, some of us, on the matter of law, and I well remember an enthusiastic freshman, who was a fellow pupil at the pleader's with whom I was to carry on my studies afterwards, rushing from the room in which he read into another, which served for another set of learners, with a wild inquiry: " Will some gentleman here—if any—oblige me with the difference between an indorser and an indorsee?" There was plenty of variety for me, certainly, to the student side of the pleader-days. There were much of society and of dancing into the small hours, with many a waltz with an enthusiastic and well-suited partner. Years afterwards, when in the States, I met and made friends with the famous Mrs. Julia Ward Howe. We fell into a transcendental discussion, in which I did my best to hold my speculative part. "What," at last said my interested interlocutor, " what, on the whole, do you think is the greatest sensation of pleasure that a human being may be capable of experiencing?" "I can tell you without hesitation/' I answered And the lady looked for true enlightenment " It is, my dear Mrs. Ward Howe, a waltz with a perfect partner, to perfect music, on a perfect floor!11 Mrs. Ward Howe looked staggered for a moment, coming, as the argument did, with the greater force, because the scene was a ball in the public rooms at Newport But her readiness was equal to the occasion, and the feminine side was uppermost at once. " Do you really think so? My daughter loves waltzing. May I introduce you ? " The result of that dance was a visit of some few days to the Howes' cottage hard by Newport, in the true American summer heat, and an introduction to the pleasure of the hammock and cooling drinks under masterful home treatment, varied as far as possible by our experiments in philosophical inquiry, which would assume shapes both practical and interesting in the hands of Mrs. Julia Ward Howe.

But the London-time of early manhood own account a great delight to the votary of the older game. But the new strengths turned out to mean winning. and in the end what wins pays. Tennis and crickei could never be reduced to the almost mechanical precision of chess or of whist in the bands of masters, so the old methods went by the board. The last time I saw the wonderful Barre, who could set a basket in the middle of the court and undertake to step into it between every two strokes he played, so completely was he master of his implements, it was athetic enough. Very weak and ill after the siege, he was seated in the *dedans* one day at Lord's, watching a fight between two champions of the new school with a puzzled face. When some very strong stroke was sent down, an enthusiastic votary of the modems called out, "Ah ! Barre could never have made a stroke like that !" The old chap overheard it, and said, with a quiet sadness that moved us a great deal, "II a raison. Je ne puis plus rien prouver maintenant. "

www.bookjungle.com *email: sales@bookjungle.com fax: 630-214-0564 mail: Book Jungle PO Box 2226 Champaign, IL 61825*

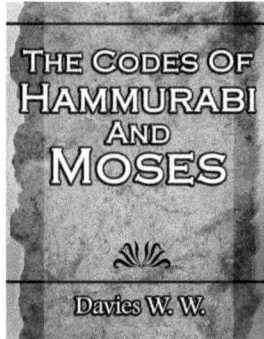

The Codes Of Hammurabi And Moses
W. W. Davies

QTY

The discovery of the Hammurabi Code is one of the greatest achievements of archaeology, and is of paramount interest, not only to the student of the Bible, but also to all those interested in ancient history...

Religion   **ISBN:** *1-59462-338-4*   **Pages:132**
MSRP $12.95

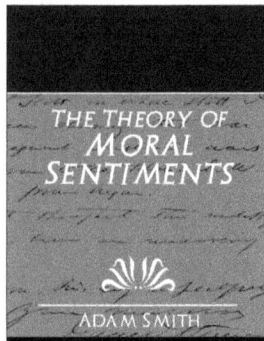

The Theory of Moral Sentiments
Adam Smith

QTY

This work from 1749. contains original theories of conscience amd moral judgment and it is the foundation for systemof morals.

Philosophy **ISBN:** *1-59462-777-0*   **Pages:536**
MSRP $19.95

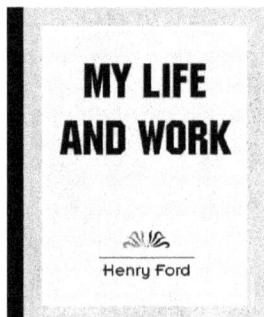

Jessica's First Prayer
Hesba Stretton

QTY

In a screened and secluded corner of one of the many railway-bridges which span the streets of London there could be seen a few years ago, from five o'clock every morning until half past eight, a tidily set-out coffee-stall, consisting of a trestle and board, upon which stood two large tin cans, with a small fire of charcoal burning under each so as to keep the coffee boiling during the early hours of the morning when the work-people were thronging into the city on their way to their daily toil...

Pages:84

Childrens   **ISBN:** *1-59462-373-2*   *MSRP $9.95*

My Life and Work
Henry Ford

QTY

Henry Ford revolutionized the world with his implementation of mass production for the Model T automobile. Gain valuable business insight into his life and work with his own auto-biography... "We have only started on our development of our country we have not as yet, with all our talk of wonderful progress, done more than scratch the surface. The progress has been wonderful enough but..."

Pages:300

Biographies/   **ISBN:** *1-59462-198-5*   *MSRP $21.95*

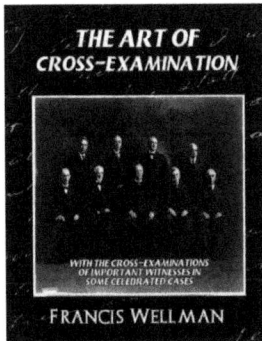

The Art of Cross-Examination
Francis Wellman

QTY

I presume it is the experience of every author, after his first book is published upon an important subject, to be almost overwhelmed with a wealth of ideas and illustrations which could readily have been included in his book, and which to his own mind, at least, seem to make a second edition inevitable. Such certainly was the case with me; and when the first edition had reached its sixth impression in five months, I rejoiced to learn that it seemed to my publishers that the book had met with a sufficiently favorable reception to justify a second and considerably enlarged edition. ...

Reference   **ISBN: *1-59462-647-2***

Pages:412

MSRP $19.95

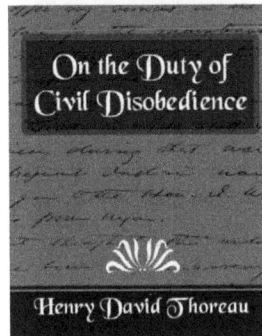

On the Duty of Civil Disobedience
Henry David Thoreau

QTY

Thoreau wrote his famous essay, On the Duty of Civil Disobedience, as a protest against an unjust but popular war and the immoral but popular institution of slave-owning. He did more than write—he declined to pay his taxes, and was hauled off to gaol in consequence. Who can say how much this refusal of his hastened the end of the war and of slavery ?

Law   **ISBN: *1-59462-747-9***

Pages:48

MSRP $7.45

Dream Psychology Psychoanalysis for Beginners
Sigmund Freud

QTY

Sigmund Freud, born Sigismund Schlomo Freud (May 6, 1856 - September 23, 1939), was a Jewish-Austrian neurologist and psychiatrist who co-founded the psychoanalytic school of psychology. Freud is best known for his theories of the unconscious mind, especially involving the mechanism of repression; his redefinition of sexual desire as mobile and directed towards a wide variety of objects; and his therapeutic techniques, especially his understanding of transference in the therapeutic relationship and the presumed value of dreams as sources of insight into unconscious desires.

Psychology   **ISBN: *1-59462-905-6***

Pages:196

MSRP $15.45

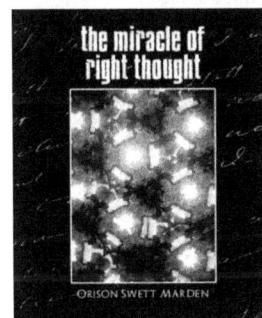

The Miracle of Right Thought
Orison Swett Marden

QTY

Believe with all of your heart that you will do what you were made to do. When the mind has once formed the habit of holding cheerful, happy, prosperous pictures, it will not be easy to form the opposite habit. It does not matter how improbable or how far away this realization may see, or how dark the prospects may be, if we visualize them as best we can, as vividly as possible, hold tenaciously to them and vigorously struggle to attain them, they will gradually become actualized, realized in the life. But a desire, a longing without endeavor, a yearning abandoned or held indifferently will vanish without realization.

Pages:360

Self Help   **ISBN: *1-59462-644-8***

MSRP $25.45

www.bookjungle.com *email: sales@bookjungle.com fax: 630-214-0564 mail: Book Jungle PO Box 2226 Champaign, IL 61825*

QTY

The Rosicrucian Cosmo-Conception Mystic Christianity *by Max Heindel* ISBN: *1-59462-188-8* **$38.95**
The Rosicrucian Cosmo-conception is not dogmatic, neither does it appeal to any other authority than the reason of the student. It is: not controversial, but is: sent forth in, hope that it may help to clear... New Age/Religion Pages 646

Abandonment To Divine Providence *by Jean-Pierre de Caussade* ISBN: *1-59462-228-0* **$25.95**
"The Rev. Jean Pierre de Caussade was one of the most remarkable spiritual writers of the Society of Jesus in France in the 18th Century. His death took place at Toulouse in 1751. His works have gone through many editions and have been republished... Inspirational/Religion Pages 400

Mental Chemistry *by Charles Haanel* ISBN: *1-59462-192-6* **$23.95**
Mental Chemistry allows the change of material conditions by combining and appropriately utilizing the power of the mind. Much like applied chemistry creates something new and unique out of careful combinations of chemicals the mastery of mental chemistry... New Age Pages 354

The Letters of Robert Browning and Elizabeth Barret Barrett 1845-1846 vol II *by Robert Browning and Elizabeth Barrett* ISBN: *1-59462-193-4* **$35.95**
  Biographies Pages 596

Gleanings In Genesis (volume I) *by Arthur W. Pink* ISBN: *1-59462-130-6* **$27.45**
Appropriately has Genesis been termed "the seed plot of the Bible" for in it we have, in germ form, almost all of the great doctrines which are afterwards fully developed in the books of Scripture which follow... Religion/Inspirational Pages 420

The Master Key *by L. W. de Laurence* ISBN: *1-59462-001-6* **$30.95**
In no branch of human knowledge has there been a more lively increase of the spirit of research during the past few years than in the study of Psychology, Concentration and Mental Discipline. The requests for authentic lessons in Thought Control, Mental Discipline and... New Age/Business Pages 422

The Lesser Key Of Solomon Goetia *by L. W. de Laurence* ISBN: *1-59462-092-X* **$9.95**
This translation of the first book of the "Lernegton" which is now for the first time made accessible to students of Talismanic Magic was done, after careful collation and edition, from numerous Ancient Manuscripts in Hebrew, Latin, and French... New Age/Occult Pages 92

Rubaiyat Of Omar Khayyam *by Edward Fitzgerald* ISBN: *1-59462-332-5* **$13.95**
Edward Fitzgerald, whom the world has already learned, in spite of his own efforts to remain within the shadow of anonymity, to look upon as one of the rarest poets of the century, was born at Bredfield, in Suffolk, on the 31st of March, 1809. He was the third son of John Purcell... Music Pages 172

Ancient Law *by Henry Maine* ISBN: *1-59462-128-4* **$29.95**
The chief object of the following pages is to indicate some of the earliest ideas of mankind, as they are reflected in Ancient Law, and to point out the relation of those ideas to modern thought. Religion/History Pages 452

Far-Away Stories *by William J. Locke* ISBN: *1-59462-129-2* **$19.45**
"Good wine needs no bush, but a collection of mixed vintages does. And this book is just such a collection. Some of the stories I do not want to remain buried for ever in the museum files of dead magazine-numbers an author's not unpardonable vanity..." Fiction Pages 272

Life of David Crockett *by David Crockett* ISBN: *1-59462-250-7* **$27.45**
"Colonel David Crockett was one of the most remarkable men of the times in which he lived. Born in humble life, but gifted with a strong will, an indomitable courage, and unremitting perseverance... Biographies/New Age Pages 424

Lip-Reading *by Edward Nitchie* ISBN: *1-59462-206-X* **$25.95**
Edward B. Nitchie, founder of the New York School for the Hard of Hearing, now the Nitchie School of Lip-Reading, Inc, wrote "LIP-READING Principles and Practice". The development and perfecting of this meritorious work on lip-reading was an undertaking... How-to Pages 400

A Handbook of Suggestive Therapeutics, Applied Hypnotism, Psychic Science *by Henry Munro* ISBN: *1-59462-214-0* **$24.95**
  Health/New Age/Health/Self-help Pages 376

A Doll's House: and Two Other Plays *by Henrik Ibsen* ISBN: *1-59462-112-8* **$19.95**
Henrik Ibsen created this classic when in revolutionary 1848 Rome. Introducing some striking concepts in playwriting for the realist genre, this play has been studied the world over. Fiction/Classics/Plays 308

The Light of Asia *by sir Edwin Arnold* ISBN: *1-59462-204-3* **$13.95**
In this poetic masterpiece, Edwin Arnold describes the life and teachings of Buddha. The man who was to become known as Buddha to the world was born as Prince Gautama of India but he rejected the worldly riches and abandoned the reigns of power when... Religion/History/Biographies Pages 170

The Complete Works of Guy de Maupassant *by Guy de Maupassant* ISBN: *1-59462-157-8* **$16.95**
"For days and days, nights and nights, I had dreamed of that first kiss which was to consecrate our engagement, and I knew not on what spot I should put my lips..." Fiction/Classics Pages 240

The Art of Cross-Examination *by Francis L. Wellman* ISBN: *1-59462-309-0* **$26.95**
Written by a renowned trial lawyer, Wellman imparts his experience and uses case studies to explain how to use psychology to extract desired information through questioning. How-to/Science/Reference Pages 408

Answered or Unanswered? *by Louisa Vaughan* ISBN: *1-59462-248-5* **$10.95**
Miracles of Faith in China Religion Pages 112

The Edinburgh Lectures on Mental Science (1909) *by Thomas* ISBN: *1-59462-008-3* **$11.95**
This book contains the substance of a course of lectures recently given by the writer in the Queen Street Hall, Edinburgh. Its purpose is to indicate the Natural Principles governing the relation between Mental Action and Material Conditions... New Age/Psychology Pages 148

Ayesha *by H. Rider Haggard* ISBN: *1-59462-301-5* **$24.95**
Verily and indeed it is the unexpected that happens! Probably if there was one person upon the earth from whom the Editor of this, and of a certain previous history, did not expect to hear again... Classics Pages 380

Ayala's Angel *by Anthony Trollope* ISBN: *1-59462-352-X* **$29.95**
The two girls were both pretty, but Lucy who was twenty-one who supposed to be simple and comparatively unattractive, whereas Ayala was credited, as her Bombwhat romantic name might show, with poetic charm and a taste for romance. Ayala when her father died was nineteen... Fiction Pages 484

The American Commonwealth *by James Bryce* ISBN: *1-59462-286-8* **$34.45**
An interpretation of American democratic political theory. It examines political mechanics and society from the perspective of Scotsman James Bryce Politics Pages 572

Stories of the Pilgrims *by Margaret P. Pumphrey* ISBN: *1-59462-116-0* **$17.95**
This book explores pilgrims religious oppression in England as well as their escape to Holland and eventual crossing to America on the Mayflower, and their early days in New England... History Pages 268

QTY

The Fasting Cure *by Sinclair Upton*   ISBN: *1-59462-222-1*   **$13.95**
In the Cosmopolitan Magazine for May, 1910, and in the Contemporary Review (London) for April, 1910, I published an article dealing with my experiences in fasting. I have written a great many magazine articles, but never one which attracted so much attention... New Age/Self Help/Health Pages 164

Hebrew Astrology *by Sepharial*   ISBN: *1-59462-308-2*   **$13.45**
In these days of advanced thinking it is a matter of common observation that we have left many of the old landmarks behind and that we are now pressing forward to greater heights and to a wider horizon than that which represented the mind-content of our progenitors...   Astrology Pages 144

Thought Vibration or The Law of Attraction in the Thought World   ISBN: *1-59462-127-6*   **$12.95**

by William Walker Atkinson   *Psychology/Religion Pages 144*

Optimism *by Helen Keller*   ISBN: *1-59462-108-X*   **$15.95**
Helen Keller was blind, deaf, and mute since 19 months old, yet famously learned how to overcome these handicaps, communicate with the world, and spread her lectures promoting optimism. An inspiring read for everyone...   Biographies/Inspirational Pages 84

Sara Crewe *by Frances Burnett*   ISBN: *1-59462-360-0*   **$9.45**
In the first place, Miss Minchin lived in London. Her home was a large, dull, tall one, in a large, dull square, where all the houses were alike, and all the sparrows were alike, and where all the door-knockers made the same heavy sound...   Childrens/Classic Pages 88

The Autobiography of Benjamin Franklin *by Benjamin Franklin*   ISBN: *1-59462-135-7*   **$24.95**
The Autobiography of Benjamin Franklin has probably been more extensively read than any other American historical work, and no other book of its kind has had such ups and downs of fortune. Franklin lived for many years in England, where he was agent...   Biographies/History Pages 332

Name	
Email	
Telephone	
Address	
City, State ZIP	

☐ **Credit Card**   ☐ **Check / Money Order**

Credit Card Number	
Expiration Date	
Signature	

Please Mail to: Book Jungle
                    PO Box 2226
                    Champaign, IL 61825
or Fax to: 630-214-0564

ORDERING INFORMATION

web: *www.bookjungle.com*
email: *sales@bookjungle.com*
fax: *630-214-0564*
mail: *Book Jungle PO Box 2226 Champaign, IL 61825*
or PayPal *to sales@bookjungle.com*

Please contact us for bulk discounts

DIRECT-ORDER TERMS

**20% Discount if You Order
Two or More Books**
Free Domestic Shipping!
Accepted: Master Card, Visa,
Discover, American Express

www.ingramcontent.com/pod-product-compliance
Lightning Source LLC
Chambersburg PA
CBHW050353100426
42739CB00015BB/3382

* 9 7 8 1 4 3 8 5 3 5 0 4 3 *